Feeling Their Pain

Feeling Their Pain

Why Voters Want Leaders Who Care

JARED MCDONALD

OXFORD
UNIVERSITY PRESS

OXFORD
UNIVERSITY PRESS

Oxford University Press is a department of the University of Oxford. It furthers
the University's objective of excellence in research, scholarship, and education
by publishing worldwide. Oxford is a registered trade mark of Oxford University
Press in the UK and certain other countries.

Published in the United States of America by Oxford University Press
198 Madison Avenue, New York, NY 10016, United States of America.

CIP data is on file at the Library of Congress
ISBN 978-0-19-769690-3 (pbk.)
ISBN 978-0-19-769689-7 (hbk.)

DOI: 10.1093/oso/9780197696897.001.0001

Paperback printed by Marquis Book Printing, Canada
Hardback printed by Bridgeport National Bindery, Inc., United States of America

For my mom, who got me into politics.
For my dad, who got me into science.

Contents

Acknowledgments

It is perhaps ironic that the roots of this book on compassion and empathy were actually born out of my love for the pitched battles, the mudslinging, and the nefarious tactics that characterize the campaigns that occur every two years in the United States. I grew up what political scientist Eitan Hersh would call a hobbyist. I tracked the polls obsessively, followed every campaign gaffe, and tried to make predictions about what would happen in November. Sure, I also did some volunteer canvassing and some organizing at my high school, but what really interested me were the battle tactics. This interest drew me to George Washington University for my undergraduate studies and led me to work after college on the 2012 presidential election as an opposition researcher.

I ultimately decided that I wanted to study public opinion and voting behavior rather than influence it directly. I went to the University of Maryland at College Park, which was lucky because it was there that I met Mike Hanmer. I think he appreciated my background in campaign politics, if for no other reason than the fact that I responded to emails within minutes rather than hours, days, or weeks (which is more typical of academics). I came in thinking I was there to learn about statistics and research design, but he pushed me to prioritize learning about politics. In particular, he suggested that I use my practical experience for inspiration on what to research. His open-door policy led to hours of discussions on why elections turn out the way they do. I came to realize that I always thought Barack Obama would win in 2012, not because of partisanship, some policy position, or even the trajectory of the economy, but because people were convinced Obama understood their problems in a way Mitt Romney simply couldn't by virtue of his wealth and privileged background. This epiphany led to the development of my theory of empathy through commonality and the book you are now reading.

At Maryland, my interest in researching compassion was nurtured by many. Of course, I owe the biggest debt of gratitude to Mike, who read countless drafts, talked with me about my experiments, and helped fund the surveys that make up the bulk of this research. Sarah Croco was one of my earliest advocates at Maryland. She remains the best writer I know, and she spent the time getting to understand how my brain worked so she could help me translate my thoughts to the page. Other members of my committee at Maryland, including Antoine Banks, Lily Mason, Fred Conrad, and Janelle Wong, offered important feedback at multiple points throughout the research process, pushing me to consider how messages of empathy might interact with the race, gender, or the background of a candidate to yield unexpected outcomes. And I owe a special thanks to Stella Rouse, Patrick Wohlfarth, and Ric Uslaner for providing feedback on my work and supporting me through departmental research grants.

Throughout my time in grad school, I was incredibly fortunate to be surrounded by smart and supportive people who provided thoughtful feedback. In particular, I thank Zack Scott, Caitlin McCulloch, Alauna Safarpour, Candace Turitto, Julian Wamble, Heather Hicks, Katti McNally, Brandon Ives, Andrew Lugg, Jé St Sume, Charlie Hunt, Nathan Lovin, and Casey Burgat. Graduate school can be an isolating time for many, but the friendships I formed at UMD were essential to my success.

Since earning my doctorate at Maryland, I have benefited from being a member of a number of vibrant academic communities. At the University of North Carolina at Charlotte, I was surrounded by faculty and staff invested in my success. Portions of this book received crucial feedback from Zach Mohr, Jaclyn Piatak, and Jason Windett. I also owe thanks to Jim Walsh, Suzy Leland, and Martha Kropf for helping me refine the way I do survey experiments.

This book also improved during my time working with the Political Psychology Research Group at Stanford University. Jon Krosnick opened my eyes to several strands of research outside political science that connected directly with the concepts I was grappling with. I am thankful for the many conversations with Bo MacInnis, Catherine Chen, Natalie Neufeld, and Lisanne Wichgers about my research and ways to improve it.

And most recently, I owe a debt of gratitude to my colleagues at the University of Mary Washington. Portions of this research were presented at a talk on campus in the winter of 2022. The faculty and students pushed me to think more carefully about the ways empathy and compassion could operate in a multitude of contexts, both inside and outside of campaigns for elected office. Especially, I want to express my thanks to Rosalyn Cooperman and Steve Farnsworth for their mentorship and support. And thank you to my students, who bring a different (and more hopeful) perspective to the way our politics can operate even during these troubled times.

Over the course of conducting this research, I have been the beneficiary of helpful criticism from peers and colleagues in a number of different venues, namely at the Midwest and Southern Political Science Associations' annual conferences. Oxford University Press, and especially Angela Chnapko, also deserve a huge amount of credit for improving the arguments advanced in this book. The anonymous reviewers rolled up their sleeves and provided an incredible amount of tough but constructive feedback. They pushed me to think more clearly about the ways gender and empathy interact, and they helped me think through the ways survey experiments speak to phenomena in the real world.

The thanks I owe to those who have helped me in my professional life are considerable, but my biggest thanks go to those who have supported me personally. My parents, to whom this book is dedicated, are first and fore-most. I would not have developed an interest in politics if it weren't for sitting around the dinner table listening to them talk about what was going on in the world. My mom blended being a political junkie with being an activist truly invested in her community. Lawrence, Kansas, was a bizarre place to grow up, politically. A blue dot in an ocean of red. She never let that dissuade her from being involved. My dad was the first person to show me that you can do cool things with statistics and the right research design. He was my first math teacher, but he also taught me about hard work and perseverance. I'm further indebted to those people who helped shape me, namely my big brother, who has always been my champion, and my grandmother, who taught me what compassion looks like.

Finally, I want to thank the family I gained over the course of doing this research. My in-laws, including Amy, Steve, Kristin, Kevin, Laura, Majid, Alexa, Elise, Terri, and Rodney have been incredible cheerleaders and shared in my professional successes and frustrations. And, of course, my wife Lisa has had to put up with it all. She has been a constant source of support and encouragement, providing many (unpaid) hours of labor reading my writing and watching me do mock presentations. Moving from DC to Charlotte to San Francisco and back to DC, all in the span of about three years, was not easy and probably not what she would have done in an ideal world. But through all of that she has been a constant source of happiness, without which none of this work would have been possible.

1

Introduction

1.1 Biden and a Return to Compassionate Politics?

On August 17, 2020, the Democratic National Convention (DNC) opened in Milwaukee, Wisconsin. Known as the "unconventional convention" because of its virtual format amid the COVID-19 pandemic, it sought to cast blame for the ills of the nation on Republican President Donald Trump. The year began with the impeachment and acquittal of Trump for pressuring the Ukrainian president to help Trump's re-election by digging up negative information on the son of his eventual Democratic opponent, Joe Biden. [1] The political and social turmoil worsened with the COVID-19 pandemic, which to date had taken 170,000 American lives but would claim more than 330,000 by the year's end. The country had spent most of the year in lockdown, leading to business closures and skyrocketing unemployment. And in the midst of this, the killing of numerous Black Americans such as George Floyd and Breonna Taylor at the hands of police officers sent protesters to the streets, leading to deadly clashes and thousands of arrests.

The message from the Democrats on their opening night? The cause of America's pain was a lack of empathy emanating straight from the White House. The president had used police violence to clear peaceful protesters from a park in front of the White House for a photo opportunity in front of a boarded-up church.[2] He had denied and downplayed the dangers of COVID-19, endangering millions of American lives. And he had used his public office for personal gain. In short, the message from Democrats was that Trump was only in office to serve himself. Former First Lady Michelle Obama summed up the sentiment of the evening when she claimed that America was looking for leadership and consolation but was instead seeing "chaos, division, and a total and utter lack of empathy."

---

[1] Technically the president was impeached in December 2019, though the media focus on the impeachment and questions regarding how the Senate would handle a trial dominated well into 2020.

[2] "Police in D.C. make arrests after sweeping peaceful protesters from park with gas, shoving," *Washington Post*, June 1, 2020.

Feeling Their Pain. Jared McDonald, Oxford University Press. © Oxford University Press 2024.
DOI: 10.1093/oso/9780197696897.003.0001

Obama's message, however, was not simply that empathy was a prerequisite for being president—it was a prerequisite for fulfilling the requirements of American citizenship:

Empathy. That's something I've been thinking a lot about lately. The ability to walk in someone else's shoes, the recognition that someone else's experience has value too. Most of us practice this without a second thought. If we see someone suffering or struggling, we don't stand in judgment. We reach out. Because there but for the grace of God go I. It is not a hard concept to grasp. It's what we teach our children. . . . But right now, kids in this country are seeing what happens when we stop requiring empathy of one another. They're looking around wondering if we've been lying to them this whole time about who we are and what we truly value. They see people shouting in grocery stores, unwilling to wear a mask to keep us all safe. They see people calling the police on folks minding their own business, just because of the color of their skin. They see an entitlement that says only certain people belong here. That greed is good and winning is everything. Because as long as you come out on top, it doesn't matter what happens to everyone else.

Why did the DNC emphasize empathy? Because in 2020, the Democrats were running the man perhaps best situated to capitalize on an election centered on empathy. Unlike Donald Trump, Joe Biden had grown up in a working-class family and did not achieve great wealth during most of his adult life. In 2007, after 34 years in the U.S. Senate, Biden ranked 626 out of 639 on the list of wealthiest public officials.[3] Biden's nomination took place at a time not only of crisis but also of mourning. As a man who had lost a wife and daughter in a car crash and later a son to cancer, he was uniquely capable of connecting with others experiencing loss. That he had suffered from a childhood stutter and routinely offered his personal phone number to children similarly suffering was highlighted at the DNC and served to reinforce the message that Biden could draw from his personal experiences to fight for the little guy.

For viewers previously unfamiliar with Biden's compassion, the DNC was not subtle in making this message clear on its opening night. "I know Joe, because he *cares* about everybody else before himself."[4] "I believe Joe

---

[3] This is according to a 2019 Politifact report ("Fact-checking Joe Biden's claim that he was among the poorest in government"), which also noted that Biden's wealth did not increase greatly during his years as vice president.

[4] TAPS Military Mentor Kevin Penn.

Biden has the experience, the platform, and the *empathy* to build America back better."[5] "Joe Biden is somebody who deeply cares about people. People who are marginalized, who were being left behind, who are being ignored."[6] Speaker after speaker told stories of Joe Biden comforting the families of fallen soldiers or those who lost loved ones to cancer. Across all four nights of the convention, the theme of empathy, compassion, and character was tied to the Biden biography and his record on the issues.

In the aftermath of the 2020 election, many who had supported Biden claimed his victory meant a return of compassion to the presidency and a vindication for the value voters placed on matters of character. Fighting through tears, CNN political commentator Van Jones reacted to the news of Biden's victory by proclaiming "It's easier to be a parent . . . it's easier to tell your kids, character matters. Telling the truth matters. Being a good person matters."[7] Writing for *Time* magazine, author Stephanie Land wrote that Americans had "been bullied by an administration that lacks any semblance of compassion," but that Biden would "bring back the dignity in simply being human."[8] In their estimation, 2020 was a test of the character of the nation, and America had passed.

In this book, I examine those factors that lead individuals to view politicians as truly caring about people like them. In doing so, however, I note that perceptions of compassion are not as warm and fuzzy as the quotes above suggest. Unlike the conventional view of compassion as normatively good, perceptions of compassion in politics are self-interested and must therefore be viewed through a different normative lens. At times, perceptions of compassion can be cultivated in a normatively positive way. When a politician claims to care for those who are struggling, those who need help, or those who are marginalized, the compassion being conveyed is inclusive and positive. Yet perceptions of compassion can also be cultivated in exclusionary ways. Contrary to the claims of Biden supporters, many Americans *did* view Donald Trump as compassionate. Not because he cared about all people, per se, but because he cared about people *like them.*

[5] High school teacher Kori Fernandez.
[6] Senator Kirsten Gillibrand.
[7] Van Jones, CNN, November 6, 2020.
[8] Stephanie Land, "Joe Biden, Kamala Harris, and the return of empathy when America needs it most," *Time*, November 7, 2020.

The argument advanced in this book is twofold. First, I make the case that voters care about the character of their elected officials. They want leaders who are strong and decisive, but they also want leaders who can put themselves in the shoes of the voter and intuit their needs. This assertion is not new, but it often gets overlooked in an era when the conventional wisdom is that deep partisan ties are the dominant force in political behavior and other factors are essentially random noise. I do not discount the importance that partisanship plays in determining the votes of many, but note that perceptions of candidate compassion can play important, often decisive, roles in American elections.

Second, I develop and test a theory to explain why some politicians are perceived as more compassionate than others. I argue that compassion is conveyed most effectively to voters through a commonality that binds the politician with the citizen. Just as Biden conveyed his capacity for compassion through his personal experiences with loss, many politicians make relatively universal appeals to voters by conveying aspects of their biographies that make them relatable. I refer to this as *experiential empathy*, but commonalities can also be conveyed through shared emotions and shared identities. Through shared emotions, politicians convey that they *feel* the same way citizens do about the issues facing the country. This likely drove much of Donald Trump's appeal in 2016 as he spoke to an anger toward status quo politics felt deeply within the Republican base. And through shared salient identities, politicians convey an experiential link to voters without discussing specific experiences. By sharing a common race, gender, religion, or other important identity, candidates send messages about the groups of people who are likely to be first and foremost in their minds.

To be clear, the commonalities I discuss must be relevant for American politics. A politician who tries to relate to a struggling working mother by describing a time he lost a family member may not be perceived as compassionate because the experiences are too disparate. A candidate who is angry not at government but at some political enemy may not appeal to an electorate who does not share this view. And a woman seeking public office may not be viewed as empathetic by other women if those women do not consider gender to be a salient political identity. As I develop the theory of empathy through commonality throughout this book, I focus on those commonalities for which there is good reason to believe they are politically relevant to at least some, if not all, voters.

1.2 Self-Interested Compassion: Defining Key Terms

As shocking as it may be to casual observers who view elected officials as egomaniacal (or at least self-centered), Americans really *do* want political leaders who are compassionate. Yet when we hear the word "compassion," it evokes heartwarming images of providing shelter to the homeless and feeding the hungry. In the realm of electoral politics, perceptions of compassion are not about altruism, but self-interest. Voters want to know if a politician cares about people like them. In a political system that often operates as a zero-sum game, compassion conveyed to one group may alienate another. This has only worsened in recent years, as social sorting and affective polarization have left Americans so divided that the political opposition has become the enemy (Bishop and Cushing 2009; Iyengar, Sood, and Lelkes 2012; Mason 2018).

Yet past scholarship too frequently treats compassion in a politician as an intrinsically valuable character trait without determining why citizens want it in a leader or examining how citizens go about determining a politician has it. Prior research treats compassion as a trait, something a leader either has or lacks. This conjures a sense that politicians are either saints or sinners, concerned with either improving the lives of the common citizen or hungry for power and prestige. With this research, I view compassion as a state: something that a politician may possess in one situation but not in another, and something that one voter sees in a politician while another does not. Through the importance of commonality, I explain why some politicians are perceived as more compassionate than others and provide a rationale for why Americans find this characteristic desirable.

Central to this theory is the distinction between those candidates who convey sympathy and those who convey empathy. Both sympathy and empathy may be defined as types of compassion (or caring), but they are not equal in the eyes of voters. Sympathy is the act that comes with caring for another. A sympathetic person is moved outwardly to help someone they feel needs it. Empathy is the ability of one person to feel the same way another feels (or is expected to feel). Although someone may be empathetic without being sympathetic (and vice versa), these two concepts are closely related.

These definitions draw on a hotly contested debate across cognitive psychology, social psychology, and neuroscience literatures. For example, a number of prominent scholars working in social psychology treat empathy as an umbrella term that encompasses both sympathy and compassion (e.g.,

Batson, Fultz, and Schoenrade 1987; Davis 1983). Batson (1991) discusses "empathic concern," which he describes as "feeling for" another person. Others view "feeling for" as fitting the definition of sympathy, while empathy is best described as "feeling *as*" another, or the ability to take someone else's perspective (Hein and Singer 2008). For the purposes of the present research, which concerns *perceptions* of compassion rather than true compassion, it is necessary to distinguish between those emotions that make us reach outward (sympathy) and those that make us look inward (empathy), which is why I differentiate the two and explain these concepts in more detail in Chapter 3.

In many cases, scholars find, empathy is a precondition for sympathy (Batson 1987). This explains why politicians who convey empathy, as I show, are perceived as more compassionate. When a politician seeks to convey sympathy, they will claim to care about Americans (or subgroups of Americans) and promise to better their lives. Often, this will involve some tangible policy outcome. In other words, the sympathetic politician will focus on the outward action they will take and express a desire to help. An empathetic politician, by contrast, may make similar claims about action but will find a common bond with the voters that lends her claims credibility. Observers noted that Biden was especially skilled in this regard. During the economic crisis of 2008 while campaigning as the vice-presidential nominee and later as president in the wake of COVID-19, Biden relied heavily on the example of his father's struggles to find adequate employment. "My dad—he used to lie awake at night when I was a kid, staring at the ceiling, unable to sleep because he was worried about whether or not he was about to lose his healthcare, or whether we were going to have the money to pay the mortgage."[9] These words showed, as Biden would claim, that he understood that "work is more than a paycheck. It's dignity. It's respect."[10] And Biden's empathetic claims went beyond financial or economic concerns. When it was reported that President Trump called members of the military who had died in wars "losers" and "suckers,"[11] Biden confronted him on this issue by making it personal: "When my son volunteered to join the United States military, as the attorney general, and went to Iraq for the year—won the bronze star and other commendations—he wasn't a sucker." By using emotion and making issues of the economy and defense not abstract policy issues but personal

---

[9] White House remarks by President Biden on the American Rescue Plan and Signing of Executive Orders, January 22, 2021.
[10] "Father's Tough Life an Inspiration for Biden," *New York Times*, October 23, 2008.
[11] "Trump: Americans who died in war are 'losers' and 'suckers,'" *The Atlantic*, September 3, 2020.

ones, Biden conveyed a deeper level of understanding than someone who lacked a direct connection. He chose not to focus on his policy proposals to help the unemployed or military families but on his personal motivation for providing aid.

This commonality suggests that politicians can more easily put themselves in the shoes of another and will be more motivated to solve the problems people face. Yet this conceptualization is, in some ways, counterintuitive. After all, voters are looking for action, which is the hallmark of a truly sympathetic candidate. Yet the perception of sympathy is different from actually being sympathetic. A politician who claims to care and proposes specific policies to help others may face a skeptical public that understands the incentive politicians face to feign compassion. Instead, politicians who make empathetic appeals will be more successful in overcoming the skepticism of American voters.

Empathy, as I show, can be perceived in various ways. A key feature of my theory is a more expansive conceptualization of political empathy that involves a classification scheme for how voters come to view a politician as truly caring about people like them: a shared experience, a shared emotion, or a shared identity. Although Donald Trump may have lacked many common experiences to link himself to working-class voters, it was through shared emotion, I argue, that he found a connection with voters who came from financial backgrounds immensely different from his.

1.3 Trump and the Paradox of Emotional Empathy

> I'm an angry voter, how 'bout that? I'm angry about the way the country is working for the blue-collar worker.
>
> —Dave Williams, Cement Finishers Local 179[12]

> There are few places that have been more devastated by our trade policies than Pittsburgh . . . I'm angry at our leaders for being so damn stupid.
>
> —Donald Trump[13]

---

[12] "Super Tuesday II: Clinton sweeps Florida, Illinois, Ohio and North Carolina; Rubio quits after Trump wins Florida," *Washington Post*, March 15, 2016.
[13] Donald Trump speech in Pittsburgh, PA, April 13, 2016.

Although Biden's victory in the 2020 election fits the narrative that compassion matters, Americans viewed Biden as only marginally more compassionate than Donald Trump. Trump, for the many instances in which he appeared aloof, disinterested, or downright hostile toward the welfare of some Americans, received more than 74 million votes and 46.9% of the overall vote share in 2020. Although these numbers were not enough to win, both Trump's raw vote total and his vote share percentage were higher than they had been in 2016.

And this says nothing of the fact that Trump won in 2016. In the aftermath of that election, many political pundits openly questioned how such an outcome was even possible. Critics struggled to understand how Trump could spar with everyone from Republican Speaker of the House Paul Ryan to a gold star family speaking about their son, a fallen U.S. army captain, and still prevail. *Vanity Fair* summed up the feelings of many when they ran a column simply entitled, "Oh God, How Did This Happen?"

Yet for all the handwringing and head-scratching that followed the surprising outcome of the election, the quote from union worker Dave Williams helps illuminate an important reason why Donald Trump was able to hold together a winning electoral coalition. Trump conveyed his anger toward status quo politics, an anger that so many Republicans in the past seemed to lack. Many white working-class voters saw in Trump a man willing to fight for the ideals they valued—someone who would not bend to the political establishment.

The personal connection that existed between Trump and blue-collar voters might seem counterintuitive at first. Donald Trump was not known for his humble beginnings. Trump grew up in a wealthy family, achieved success in business largely through the help of his father, and had lived his life in the public eye as a billionaire developer and reality TV star. Through his bravado and gold-plated lifestyle, Trump never tried to portray himself as the "common man" with working-class roots. Yet for all the apparent disconnect with average Americans, Trump exuded an anger and disgust with status quo politics that connected with people who had backgrounds that differed greatly from his.

Of course, empathetic connections with white working-class voters made through a shared anger toward the political world will not appeal to all and can risk alienating other voters who do not belong to those groups. It was Khizr Khan, the father of fallen U.S. Army Captain Humayun Khan, who claimed that Trump was unqualified to be president of the United States because he was "without empathy for its citizens."[14] Trump's criticism of the Khan family drew widespread condemnation from both sides of the political divide. Trump's demand for a registry of Muslims living in the United States, his insistence on a border wall, and recorded comments he made regarding his ability to get away with uninvited advances toward women gave many observers the impression he was incapable of compassion toward less privileged Americans. This apparent disregard for others, coupled with his lifetime living in enormous wealth, left him with a limited base of voters to which his anger could appeal.

Yet Trump was facing an opponent in Hillary Clinton who had spent decades in politics and similarly faced questions of trustworthiness. Trump was rich, but it wasn't as though Hillary Clinton was poor. By 2014, Hillary and Bill Clinton had capitalized on their political fame to the tune of roughly $110 million.[15] Furthermore, Hillary Clinton had earned some of that wealth giving highly paid speeches to various Wall Street financial institutions. Her unwillingness to disclose the content of those speeches and the criticism that followed cast suspicion on her sincerity and willingness to work for the common person,[16] something I explore in greater detail in Chapter 5. Ultimately, Clinton did not do what Trump or Biden did in 2020. She failed to connect with her audience on a personal or emotional level. While Biden could connect through personal experience and Trump could incite via anger toward the Washington elite, Clinton was part of that same Washington elite. She was, therefore, less able to connect with voters.

The appeal of Trump's anger is apparent in the feelings of those who supported him, especially early on in the campaign. In 2016, the American National Election Studies (ANES) asked voters in the primary how often Donald Trump and Hillary Clinton made people feel angry. Unsurprisingly, a large portion of individuals (around 40%) who voted in the primaries claimed the leading candidate of the opposing party "always" made them angry.

Figure 1.1 shows that anger toward the opposing party's candidate was much more strongly associated with Republican primary voters' support for Trump than it was for Clinton in the Democratic primary. Among GOP

---

[14] Khizr Khan interview by *Meet the Press*, NBC, July 31, 2016.

[15] "How Hillary and Bill Clinton parlayed decades of public service into vast wealth," *Fortune*, February 15, 2016.

[16] "Mrs. Clinton, and your speeches?," *USA Today*, May 15, 2016.

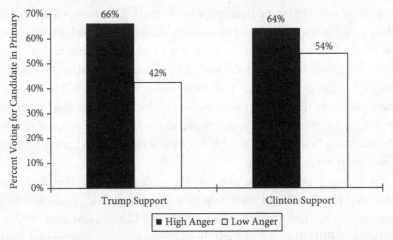

Figure 1.1 Support for Trump or Clinton in the 2016 Primary by Anger Toward the Opposition Candidate

Source: 2016 American National Election Studies (numbers represent weighted frequencies)

primary voters, those who said they were always angry with Hillary Clinton voted for Trump by a two-to-one margin. In contrast, only 42% of those who said they were less angry with Clinton said they supported Trump in the primary.

In the case of Clinton, however, anger played only a modest role. Those who claimed to be angry with Trump did support Clinton at higher rates (64% to 54%), yet the 10-percentage-point gap is less than half the 24-percentage-point gap among GOP primary voters. Trump's support was more dependent on the anger he exuded, which connected with the Republican base. Clinton, who did not show that same anger, was far less reliant on it for support.

Moreover, when Donald Trump attacked people like the Khan family and later Alicia Machado, both immigrants to the United States, it served as a signal to many voters that he was going to favor white Americans and white interests over those of other groups. Research on white identity (Jardina 2019) has shown that an increasing number of white Americans see politics in racial terms and express explicit racial bias (see Gonzalez 2020), largely due to demographic shifts and the sense of threat white Americans feel to their status in society. Trump was able to tap into this anxiety, turning it into anger and benefiting from it electorally. Two-thirds of non-college-educated whites voted for Trump in 2016, according to exit polls, the largest percentage for any candidate since 1980.[17] And as I show in Chapter 3, shared racial identities constitute an important commonality that shape perceptions of compassion, especially among white Republicans.

1.4 Compassion's Importance on Voter Behavior

Perceptions of compassion are only important insofar as they explain the existence of important features in American democracy above and beyond other factors we already know influence political behavior, such as partisanship. In these pages, I propose a new way of conceptualizing the politics of culpability and consequence. This theory accepts the argument that party ties are central to assigning blame and determining voter choice (Campbell et al. 1960; Converse [1964] 2006; Lyons and Jaeger 2014) yet recognizes that small shifts in the way the public views the particular candidates in any election can lead to large changes in electoral outcomes (MacKuen, Erikson, and Stimson 1992; Stimson 1991). I argue that a substantial number of voters cast ballots based on perceptions of compassion, where in some cases the candidate's ability to project an image of caring for citizens may trump specific policy proposals in terms of winning voters. In other cases, matters of compassion can be wedded to specific policy proposals, allowing candidates to tie their motivation for achieving a policy goal to their deep desire to help others who are like them. In the conversations I had with campaign professionals over the course of conducting this research, I noticed how the campaigns themselves would look for opportunities to project an image of caring and malign the motives of their opponents by tying compassion (or a lack thereof) to the policy positions of the candidates.

The developments of the last 30 years in American political behavior make investigating the role of compassion crucial to understanding the election outcomes we see today and are likely to see in the future. Much of the scholarship in recent decades rightly focuses on the impact of partisanship on political behavior. Despite the important role partisanship has historically played in determining voter choice and general attitudes toward political actors (Campbell et al. 1960), the rise in sociopolitical sorting has left Americans both deeply and evenly divided (e.g., Mason 2013, Bishop and

---

[17] Pew Research Center, "Behind Trump's victory: Divisions by race, gender, education," November 9, 2016.

Cushing 2009). Although the parties increasingly view each other with antipathy, pure independent voters (those who do not lean toward one party or another) remain a substantial portion of the American electorate. This group is further alienated by the viciousness displayed by the two parties toward one another (Klar and Krupnikov 2016). Given the lack of a partisan lens and the relatively low levels of interest in politics, independent voters are more likely to fall back on character evaluations of the politicians in the selection of a candidate. And because the two partisan camps are so evenly divided, the roughly 15% of voters who do not lean toward either the Democratic or Republican Parties become vitally important in determining the outcome of elections. As a result, more research is needed to examine the preferences of the relatively small number of persuadable voters who decide many political contests.

Although partisanship explains some variation in perceptions of compassion among those with partisan attachments, this relationship is far from deterministic. Some Republicans are willing to view the Democratic candidate as more compassionate, and some Democrats are willing to do the same for the Republican candidate. With the rise of social sorting, which generates both an increased preference for one's own group and a negative affect for the out-group (Mason 2018), the importance of compassion toward people *like you* is even more important today than it was in eras of low polarization. This is particularly true in primaries, where issue differences are minor, and the debate can often center on issues of character or who will be the strongest and most vociferous advocate for one group or another. As a result, the dimension of empathy dealing with identity has become an increasingly important component of public opinion toward political leaders.

I have focused thus far on 2020 and 2016 as prime examples of elections in which compassion played an important, potentially decisive, role. Yet these contests were not exceptional in terms of the important role a personal connection played in voting decisions. Figure 1.2 plots what I call the "Democratic Compassion Advantage" from the ANES and election results. This measures the degree to which the Democrat is perceived as more compassionate than the Republican in a given presidential election. Each scale runs from 1 to 5, so the resulting difference measure runs from −4 to 4. Since 1992, the Democratic candidate has always been perceived as at least somewhat more compassionate than the Republican, but the margin of the compassion advantage correlates with an important shift in electoral fortunes.

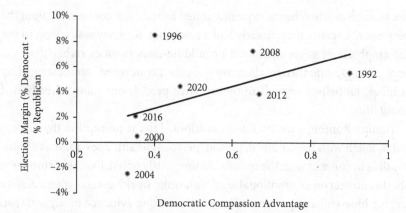

Figure 1.2 Democratic Compassion Advantage and Electoral Outcomes, 1992–2020

Source: 1992–2020 American National Election Studies (values represent weighted estimates)

Figure 1.2 suggests that being perceived as relatively more compassionate than your opponent can garner you more than 4 percentage points in the margin of the election. This is only a crude measure of compassion's effect on elections and not sufficient to establish a causal relationship between the two (analyses designed with this in mind are employed in Chapter 2), but it is notable that this 4-point swing would be enough to change the winner of the popular vote in four of the last eight presidential elections.[18]

In a number of the elections examined in this research, political observers noted the important role compassion and, more specifically, empathy played in determining the outcomes. The 2012 election was particularly noteworthy, as numerous gaffes committed by Mitt Romney helped political opponents paint him as an out-of-touch or aloof technocrat.[19] Romney had a long history in business, working for the private equity firm Bain Capital. He had tried to frame this track record as one of saving failing companies, but opponents criticized Romney throughout the primaries for his company's history of laying off workers even as it turned a profit. According to Republican primary opponents Newt Gingrich and Rick Perry, Romney was a "vulture capitalist," not a venture capitalist.[20] In the general election, he often made things

---

[18] There is also the possibility a similar shift would have changed the outcome of more elections in the electoral college.

[19] Niall Ferguson, "Romney is the technocrat candidate, but he's politically clueless," *Newsweek*, January 23, 2012.

[20] "Newt Gingrich: Bain Capital 'undermined capitalism,' killed jobs," *The Hill*, January 10, 2012.

worse, such as when he ineloquently stated he was "not concerned about the very poor" because they already had a safety net. Romney was trying to put the emphasis of government aid on middle-class families rather than the very poor. Despite this, by claiming to be "not concerned" about struggling families, he helped crystallize the negative perceptions many already had about him.

Though Romney's wealth likely contributed to the perception that he was out of touch with the common person, personal wealth does not make it impossible to connect with the masses. As previously noted, Donald Trump was able to connect on an emotional level with white working-class voters despite lacking blue-collar experience. There is also strong evidence to suggest that, perhaps due to his personal style and demeanor, many Americans did not know Donald Trump was born wealthy. This lack of knowledge was associated with higher levels of support, mediated through the belief that he was empathetic toward others (McDonald, Karol, and Mason 2020).

The Romney example also contrasts with politicians such as George W. Bush who, like Romney, came from a background of tremendous privilege. Yet, unlike Romney, Bush had a personal style that connected with people who had backgrounds different from his. Early in the 2000 campaign, Bush portrayed himself as representing a new kind of Republican, a "compassionate conservative." His laid-back demeanor, his record improving the public education system in Texas for poor and minority students,[21] and his ability to speak Spanish when visiting Latino voters lent credibility to his claims that he was in the presidential contest to better the lives of *all* Americans rather than simply champion the cause of the business community, of which he was a part.

In 2004, Bush was further juxtaposed by John Kerry, a man who was painted as an out-of-touch wealthy windsurfing New England elitist, making it easier for Bush to continue cultivating the perception he was the "compassionate conservative" fighting for the values of everyday Americans. Although Democrats are generally perceived to be, on average, more compassionate than Republicans, the 2004 election represents the smallest Democratic compassion advantage for all presidential elections from 1992 to 2020 (see Figure 1.2). Not coincidentally, George W. Bush's re-election in 2004 also represents the only instance in the data I examine where a Republican won the national

---

[21] "ON THE RECORD: Governor Bush and education; turnaround in Texas schools looks good for Bush in 2000," *New York Times*, May 28, 1999.

popular vote. Bush himself may have learned about the importance of connecting with voters on an emotional level by watching his father lose out to the more empathetic Bill Clinton, who famously told one critic "I feel your pain."[22] In contrast to the 2004 election where the Democrat's advantage on compassion was relatively narrow, Clinton's victory in 1992 represented the largest gap in the last 30 years.

Examples such as these appear in nearly every presidential campaign and naturally receive attention from the media. Kendall (1995, 2000) shows that the media is drawn to stories about the personalities of the candidates for office, which are often simpler and easier to understand for a broad audience. As part of Chapter 2, I examine the ways campaigns seek to cultivate an image of caring through the media. I also interview a number of Republican and Democratic campaign operatives to explore the context in which voters perceive a politician as caring or unfeeling. With these analyses, it becomes clear that campaigns consider perceptions of personality traits, namely those regarding compassion, essential for winning over voters. These analyses also reveal the special importance perceptions of compassion have among Democrats in particular. Because the Democratic Party is perceived to be relatively stronger on questions of caring and compassion (Hayes 2005), Democratic campaigns are generally more eager to make compassion the defining character trait of any election.

In more recent decades, political scientists have also begun to examine the important effect perceptions of compassion have on voting decisions. The literature on political behavior and character traits finds strong evidence that voter perceptions of empathy, integrity, competence, and leadership influence voter choice and a host of other politically relevant measures of public support (Goren 2002, 2007; Holian and Prysby 2015; Kinder 1986; McCann 1990). Empathy stands out among these character traits, not because the others are unimportant, but because empathy is the only one that has been traditionally defined by self-interest. Political scientists seeking to understand questions of compassion and empathy ask citizens if politicians "care about people like you," instead of asking whether the politician is caring in general. This provides stronger theoretical reasons to suspect that perceptions of compassion will be higher in specific circumstances and to test them empirically. Moreover, research on the dimensions of morality highlight caring as one of the few moral foundations that matter to *all* Americans, not just

[22] Clinton question and answer session in New York, New York, March 27, 1992.

for liberals or conservatives. As Haidt (2012, p. 183) notes, "Everyone—left, right, and center—says that concerns about compassion, cruelty, fairness, and injustice are relevant to their judgments about right and wrong," whereas concerns about loyalty, authority, and purity are more exclusively the concern of American conservatives. Understanding why some politicians are perceived as compassionate while others are not is, therefore, paramount in explaining why some campaigns are successful while others are not.

1.5 Overview of the Book

Before developing a theory for why some politicians are perceived to be more compassionate than others, I first must demonstrate that these perceptions ultimately influence voting decisions and election outcomes. In Chapter 2, I therefore demonstrate the importance of these perceptions by investigating the sometimes decisive role they play in voter choice. Even after accounting for a host of factors known to influence voting decisions, perceptions of compassion consistently exert an independent influence on individuals' voting behavior. I show that compassion matters by focusing on both the supply (the campaigns) and the demand (the voters) sides of candidate character. Using elite interviews with campaign professionals and the speeches of major candidates for the presidency in the last 20 years, I show that the campaigns often seek to drive a narrative that their opponent is unfeeling toward the average person. In the interviews, Democrats are much quicker to discuss the need to appear compassionate and, conversely, to paint their opposition as lacking in compassion. I support this claim further by leveraging data on campaign speeches. Using a text analysis of over 3,300 presidential campaign speeches from 2000 to 2020 (Scott 2021), I show that Democratic presidential candidates more often use language related to caring and compassion. Using high-quality survey data, I estimate the effect perceptions of compassion have on voter choice in multiple electoral contexts. These analyses demonstrate the importance perceptions of compassion have on voter choice, which is especially pronounced among independent voters and partisan voters in primaries. In situations where the partisan lens is not active, perceptions of compassion have special influence.

In Chapter 3, I turn to examining those factors that influence perceptions of compassion. To do this, I develop a theory of political compassion and present evidence to support the assertion that compassion is effectively conveyed through commonality. I begin by noting that, although citizens may want sympathetic political leaders, promises of caring are deemed more credible if they come with an empathic bond. The key feature behind the theory of compassion I develop is the typology for the relevant commonalities politicians have at their disposal when messaging around themes of empathy: experience, emotion, and identity. The experiments I rely on show that empathetic messages outperform sympathetic ones in boosting perceptions that a candidate truly "cares about people like you." These studies leverage the same sorts of personal stories political candidates themselves use in campaign speeches. In examining the important role empathy plays in developing positive perceptions of compassion, I test the three pathways to empathy and discuss the ways experience, emotion, and identity might interact. This approach recognizes that there are numerous methods a candidate has for revealing herself as empathetic that go far beyond personal experience.

In Chapter 4, I consider how gender and parenthood shape perceptions of political character. This recognizes that compassion is often a gendered trait, "owned" by women and connected to stereotypically maternal concepts of warmth and nurturing. Yet, drawing on the literature in sociology, social psychology, and gender studies, I argue that gender identity overall gives an advantage to male candidates for office. Although women seeking public office are perceived as compassionate, this places them in a double-bind. They are expected to emphasize compassion, so they are viewed less favorably when they opt instead to convey messages related to leadership. And although parents may be perceived as more compassionate by others who are also parents, this is true for both mothers and fathers, and as such does not offer women seeking office a special advantage. I support these claims with two behavioral survey experiments. On the one hand, I find that although women receive no additional boost for conveying messages of caring, they are punished for going "against type" by conveying leadership. Men, on the other hand, receive a boost in favorability when they convey messages of caring. Thus, women are severely constrained in the types of messages and likely the types of policies they can champion. Consistent with the theory of empathy through commonality, I find that parents prefer candidates who are also parents, and that those individuals who are high in gender identity also prefer politicians who represent them descriptively.

Whereas Chapters 3 and 4 suggest several strategies for campaigns and candidates seeking to convince voters they are empathetic, in Chapter 5

I recognize that smear campaigns often seek to do the opposite. Drawing from the literature on negative ads and character attacks, I reason that if empathetic appeals can increase support for a candidate, criticism can likewise damage these perceptions and depress support. Using an experiment administered during the 2016 presidential election, I show that negative attacks made against Hillary Clinton damaged evaluations of her candidacy. But I also show that there are strategies campaigns can use to mitigate the effect of these attacks. Because evaluations of compassion are a comparative exercise (i.e., is a candidate more/less empathetic than her opponent), attacks on Clinton were less effective if they were accompanied by a similar attack on Donald Trump.

Finally, in Chapter 6 I discuss the broader implications of this research, both for political scientists and political professionals trying to engage a sometimes apathetic or misinformed electorate. Although mudslinging and negative campaigning are unlikely to vanish any time soon, my research suggests that appearing broadly empathetic is one of only a few ways politicians today can effectively reach across the aisle and build broad electoral coalitions. In many ways, empathy offers a chance to depolarize an extremely skeptical and divided electorate.

2

Who Cares? Why Compassion Matters in the Era of Polarization

I could stand in the middle of Fifth Avenue and shoot somebody, and I wouldn't lose voters.

—Donald J. Trump[1]

In the modern era of highly polarized partisan politics, quotes like this one from then-candidate for president Donald Trump strike many as credible evidence that compassion must not matter to Americans when it comes time to vote. How else could a politician claim that he could shoot someone and not lose votes, and then win the presidency less than a year later? I demonstrate in this chapter that, despite the quote above, perceptions of compassion exert a tremendous amount of influence on election outcomes. In fact, the deeply and evenly divided partisan electorate creates an environment in which perceptions of compassion can play an outsized, often pivotal role in electoral politics.

Trump's assertion that he could shoot someone and not lose votes, while hyperbolic, reflects the consensus among political scientists that most voting decisions are determined long before the parties have even selected candidates for the general election. Voting decisions often come down to partisanship, a stable attachment that serves as a lens through which citizens view political events (e.g., Campbell et al. 1960). Partisan sorting and affective polarization have created party coalitions that are not only sharply, but evenly, divided both in government and in the electorate (Lee 2016; Mason 2018). Can we imagine a modern presidential election in which one of the major party candidates failed to win at least 45% of the two-party vote? In 2008, facing one of the worst economies in the past century and after eight years of having a Republican in the White House, John McCain still managed to garner 46% of the popular vote. And

[1] Trump campaign rally in Sioux Center, IA, January 23, 2016.

Feeling Their Pain. Jared McDonald, Oxford University Press. © Oxford University Press 2024.
DOI: 10.1093/oso/9780197696897.003.0002

despite prognostications that "Never Trump" Republicans would bolt the Republican Party, cratering support for Donald Trump, he still received a similar 46% of the overall popular vote in 2016 and improved upon that in 2020, receiving nearly 47% of all votes during a global pandemic and economic downturn. Recent elections have seen a tightening of both the floor and ceiling of popular vote share between the Democrats and Republicans. In this electoral environment, few votes are up for grabs each November, but those votes that are persuadable become even more critical in determining who wins and who loses. It is in those situations where partisanship is not a useful cue (e.g., among independent voters, partisan voters in primaries) that perceptions of compassion should play an even more important role.

To make the case that compassion matters to voters, I begin by addressing the literature on voter choice and electoral accountability, identifying how past research has situated perceptions of candidate character among the litany of factors thought to influence election outcomes. To assess whether compassion is still an important factor for voters, I begin by listening to the voters themselves. From election to election, when asked what qualities they look for in a president, voters consistently claim they want a candidate who cares about people like them. This is particularly true for Democratic voters, who frequently cite compassion as being one of the top qualities in a candidate for office. Second, I rely on interviews with campaign professionals and a textual analysis from presidential speeches to show that the campaigns and candidates believe personal character is central to winning elections. Finally, I rely on observational data to estimate the effect of compassion on individual voting decisions, paying special attention to independent voters in general elections and partisans in primary elections. Using data collected around presidential elections by the American National Election Studies (ANES) from 1992 to 2020, I find that perceptions of candidate compassion vary a great deal, even when the voters and the candidate share the same party. I find that this variation strongly predicts voter choice in recent presidential elections, especially among independent voters. And using a survey of voters in the State of Maryland during a hotly contested Senate primary, I find that perceptions of compassion were strongly correlated with voter choice among primary voters. These data also provide evidence that shared racial identity is a major driver in perceptions of compassion in American elections, which I explore further using experimental evidence in Chapter 3.

2.1 Partisan Polarization and Models
of Electoral Accountability

Any attempt to study electoral behavior has rightly recognized the critical role of political parties in shaping attitudes toward policies and candidates for office. For the better part of a century, scholars have found that partisanship is transmitted through childhood and early adulthood socialization, and it frequently persists as a lens through which individuals view political events (Berelson, Lazarsfeld, and McPhee 1954; Campbell et al. 1960; Green, Palmquist, and Schickler 2002). Despite an era in which scholars argued that the role of parties had diminished (Niemi and Weisberg 1976; Smith 1988; Burnham 1989), by the 2000s the importance of parties had once again become central to studies of voting decisions and political behavior more broadly (e.g., Bartels 2000b).

Yet recent research no longer views partisanship as stemming primarily from childhood and early adulthood socialization; rather, it is an identity generated by an overlapping set of salient social identities. The political realignment beginning in the 1960s has led to "well-sorted" parties, meaning greater homogeneity (Bishop and Cushing 2009). As the parties have homogenized, partisan attachments became more deeply entrenched, and partisan victories or losses have become more important (e.g., Fiorina and Abrams 2008; Iyengar, Sood, and Lelkes 2012; Mason 2014, 2018). Partisan sorting and affective political polarization force us to reconsider whether American political behavior can be properly understood through a framework of policy preferences (Downs 1957), retrospective evaluations of politicians' performance (Abramowitz, Lanoue, and Ramesh 1988; Ferejohn 1986; Hibbing and Alford 1981; Key 1966; Lanoue 1994; MacKuen, Erikson, & Stimson 1992; Rudolph 2003), or prospective evaluations (Kuklinski and West 1981; Lockerbie 1991).

Drawing from the literature on motivated reasoning (Kunda 1990; Taber and Lodge 2006), scholars argue that partisans perceive events in the country to be better or worse depending on whether the current president is a copartisan, essentially turning a survey item on the state of the nation into a proxy for partisanship (Redlawsk 2002). They may even use a survey item on the welfare of the nation as a whole as an opportunity to express support or opposition to the current administration, as the theory of expressive choice implies (Schuessler 2000). Political psychologists view partisanship as a social identity (Huddy and Bankert 2017; Tajfel et al. 1971) that can function even if it is devoid of true policy attitudes. It is a deep-seated preference to see the in-group victorious and the out-group defeated that motivates political engagement among those highest in this form of partisan identity (Mason 2018). From this perspective, fewer Americans are willing to receive new information on the state of the nation and assign blame to leaders rationally and dispassionately.

Compounding this problem, scholars are skeptical that American voters are competent enough to assign blame and give credit where it is due. Being the ideal civic citizen in the United States requires an individual to have basic knowledge about politics and current events and access to unbiased sources of political information. Political scientists have shown for decades, however, that the American voting public lacks basic political knowledge, suggesting that they may be unaware of the facts necessary to punish bad performance and reward good performance (Converse [1964] 2006; Delli Carpini and Keeter 1996). The information environment is often littered with misinformation (Jerit, Barabas, and Bolson 2006), and citizens seek "friendly" information environments where their pre-existing opinions are less likely to be challenged (Kuklinski et al. 2000; Kuklinski et al. 2001; Mutz 2006). In short, the extant literature on electoral accountability does not paint a flattering picture of the average American voter.

Despite the impact that partisan affective polarization has had in recent years, macroeconomic factors continue to predict election outcomes (Abramowitz 2012; Campbell 2012; Erikson and Wlezien 2012), suggesting that factors beyond partisanship continue to shape voter perceptions of candidates seeking office.

2.2 Wading into the Debate over the Importance of Candidate Traits

Prior work on partisanship and performance evaluations, while critical to our understanding of political behavior, poses something of a puzzle when we consider the electoral outcomes we often see. Scholars have recognized for more than a half century that static partisan and group attachments play a vital role in determining voter choice and public approval for elected officials. Despite these findings, the outcomes of elections continue to shift based on the changing preferences of a relatively small number of citizens. These shifts have become more meaningful as the parties have become more evenly divided, increasing the competitiveness of elections at the national level (Lee 2016). Despite the predictive power of partisanship in determining voter choice, then, we lack explanations for critical variation in public support. That Americans lack basic political knowledge and are, perhaps, unable to punish or reward political leaders rationally (Delli Carpini and Keeter 1996; see also Achen and Bartels 2016) further complicates this issue. Should we accept, then, that voting decisions at any given time come down to partisanship and a few other factors outside the control of politicians?

I argue against this view, not because I have a drastically more optimistic perspective to offer, but because this view neglects the important role voters' perceptions of the candidates play in election outcomes. In presenting this view, I borrow from Hibbing and Theiss-Morse (2002), who posit that it is unrealistic to expect Americans to have well-defined positions on a wide range of policy options. Instead, most Americans agree it is best for some legislative decisions to take place behind closed doors where well-informed experts can debate and make decisions in key areas of policy. I add to this framework by arguing that, in addition to expertise, voters also want someone making those decisions who cares about people like them, as that suggests they are trustworthy. Putting trust in someone, in this sense, is a rational behavior, as it seeks to estimate the probability that a politician will keep her promises to other people (Uslaner 2008). By promises, I am referring less to direct policy pledges candidates make during elections and more to the perception of individual citizens that the politician in question will work to help them.

Given the inability of many Americans to live up to the ideal civic citizen and their proclivity to instead cling to politically relevant social identities, it becomes far clearer why many might choose to fall back on their own ideas about the character of one candidate compared to another. Generating an impression of a candidate, accurate or not, is relatively easy in a news cycle that provides daily sound bites from the campaigns and often focuses on personal narratives. Compared to more traditional forms of electoral accountability, focusing on character traits does not require a great deal of knowledge about the issues. It also does not require that a voter has the ability to project confidently into the future about how one party's campaign promises would impact her daily life compared to another party's promises. Instead, voters must get a sense of whether the candidate cares about people like them.

Studies looking specifically at voter perceptions of compassion, however, have been sparse in recent years. Most of the seminal works on the importance of candidate character date back several decades. Fenno (1978) and

Mayhew (1974) describe in great detail the pains members of Congress take to endear themselves to constituents, in part by building empathetic bonds. Fenno in particular (1978) describes the efforts of congresspeople to convince voters they are not part of the Washington machine and have not forgotten their roots in their home district. This task has become even more difficult in recent years as partisan polarization has nationalized much of the media coverage of congressional politics, effectively ending the conventional belief that "all politics is local."[2]

Why do politicians value building empathic connections with voters? Kinder (1986) asserts that voters want to attribute motivation to the actions of a president, something that is made easier if the voter understands (or believes she understands) the type of character the president has. Kinder (1986) furthermore sets up a framework for classifying important candidate traits, including competence, leadership, integrity, and empathy.

Despite this typology, scholars have struggled to identify the precise dimensions of character as they apply to electoral politics. Some have argued for as few as two dimensions to character while others believe there are as many as six (e.g., Aaldering and Vliegenthart 2016; Greene 2001; Johnston 2002), suggesting the need for deeper theoretical development of the individual dimensions that may influence public evaluations. Yet the research in this field consistently finds that perceptions of compassion have a clear and sometimes pivotal impact on voter choice and election outcomes (Aaldering and Vliegenthart 2016; Goren 2002, 2007; McCann 1990; Miller and Shanks 1996). Still, in the context of American politics, which is characterized by strong partisanship, affective polarization, and motivated reasoning, some scholars argue the causal arrow runs in the opposite direction. Researchers working in this vein claim that perceptions of particular candidate character traits are actually an outgrowth of partisan attachments and global evaluations (Bartels 2002; Lodge and Taber 2013).

This perspective has both its advantages and drawbacks. I do not claim that evaluations of candidate compassion should be examined without consideration for factors that may influence them. Indeed, the partisanship of the voter and politician matters a great deal in determining whether someone views a candidate as compassionate. Yet this relationship is not deterministic. Furthermore, Hayes (2005)

---

[2] In more recent research, Hunt (2021) finds that having "local roots" in a congressional district increases a candidate's vote share, suggesting that candidate image remains an important factor in voting decisions.

points out that parties "own" particular traits much in the same way they "own" issue areas. While trait ownership advantages Democratic candidates on matters of compassion, Hayes and others (e.g., McCann 1990) point out that these perceptions are still malleable and candidate dependent. Though Democrats are perceived as more compassionate and Republicans are perceived as stronger leaders, the degree to which the candidates outperform expectations based on partisanship plays an important role in overall evaluations of the politicians. Republicans, then, may rate the Democrat as more compassionate, making them more likely than their co-partisans to defect in a general election.

A number of scholars have argued convincingly that if the causal arrow truly ran in the opposite direction, perceptions of candidate character traits should fit on a single dimension (i.e., the general likability of the politician). This is not what the character trait research finds (Funk 1996, 1997, 1999; Hayes 2005).

Additionally, reversing the causal arrow is theoretically unsatisfying. Arguing that individual trait evaluations are determined by global evaluations does little to explain how voters come to have these global evaluations in the first place. Making the case that voters believe a candidate is a "good person" and therefore a "compassionate leader" neglects the process by which Americans come to have a positive opinion of the politician. Looking at the process by which voters believe a candidate is compassionate and therefore a "good person" helps us better understand the bottom-up process by which voters develop positive attitudes toward politicians that ultimately result in election victories.

The argument I make here, then, does not deny the importance of static partisan attachments; instead, it shows that perceptions of compassion matter above and beyond what partisanship can explain. Indeed, if these perceptions were determined entirely by factors such as partisanship and trait ownership, we would see little variation in perceptions of compassion from one candidate to the next. Yet this is not what the data show. With each new election cycle, particular candidates are seen as relatively more or less compassionate than the candidate who came before them. Despite the difficulty modeling the complicated processes that underlie voter decisions, prior research finds evidence consistent with the notion that perceptions of compassion influence election outcomes (Campbell 1983; Goren 2002; Greene 2001; Holian and Prysby 2011, 2014, 2015; Miller, Wattenberg, and Malanchuk 1986; Miller and Shanks 1996).

While other traits (such as competence, leadership, or integrity) are worthy of greater research, I choose to focus on compassion for a number of reasons. First, the desire to have compassionate political leaders is based on the simplest of motivations: self-interest. A compassionate leader is desirable because she will be more motivated to solve the problems the voters face. Yet political scientists assert that much of what we see in voting decisions cannot be explained by a conventional conceptualization of pure self-interest, such as "pocketbook" voting decisions, forcing scholars to rethink what factors voters consider when defining their self-interest. Though scholars have argued whether heuristics are effective in leading voters to "correct" decisions (e.g., Achen and Bartels 2016; Gilovich, Griffin, and Kahneman 2002; Lupia 1994; Popkin 1994), a new line of thinking asserts that political decisions largely come down to which politically relevant group(s) one belongs (Green, Palmquist, and Schickler 2002; Mason 2018). Whether a voter chooses a party or a candidate due to a group identity or an ideological heuristic, the voter is still seeking to satisfy some conception of self-interest. And whereas candidate character traits such as leadership or integrity serve a communal interest, compassion is unique in that it is focused on the candidate's ability to care for the individual voter or those who are like the voter.

Compassion is also ripe for further research because of the crucial role it has played in the past several presidential elections and the centrality it plays in campaign messaging (explored later in this chapter). Even outside the context of an election, messages about compassion fill policy debates. The discourse about the minimum wage, healthcare, education, and taxation all take on some kind of personal moral texture. In the aftermath of the failed Republican effort to repeal the Affordable Care Act in 2017, Senator Cory Booker claimed, "We owe tonight's victory of compassion and good policy . . . to countless ordinary Americans who made an extraordinary effort to speak up and speak out against a craven attempt to leave millions of Americans without coverage."[3]

The focus by political scientists, especially in the 1980s and 1990s, on character traits made a great deal of sense in an era when political news consumers were shifting away from print media and toward television (Keeter 1987). Television offered candidates the ability to shape voter perceptions through style rather than substance. Yet these studies largely focused on the bigger picture, establishing the effect of trait evaluations on public approval and

---

[3] Senator Cory Booker press release, July 17, 2017.

voter choice. They did not attempt to explain why some politicians were seen as more compassionate, more competent, or stronger leaders.

With the introduction of social media and the ability of American politicians to communicate directly with constituents, the United States finds itself in a political and media environment that places even greater importance on a candidate's ability to directly connect with the masses and cultivate their own public persona. Donald Trump cited Twitter as one of the key factors to his victory in 2016, and most of what he conveyed on that platform was devoid of policy content. Indeed, more often Trump used the platform to convey his anger and disgust with the political establishment, which gave voters an idea for the type of person he was. Trump was one such candidate that was able to leverage new forms of communication to appeal to a partisan base that was frustrated and angry with political leaders in the United States.

2.3 Compassion and the Partisan Lens Hypothesis

As a review of the literature makes clear, studying compassion requires that a great deal of attention is paid to the role of partisanship, since it explains a large portion of voting decisions in the United States. In the context of partisan polarization, it is clear that the party ties of everyday Americans matter in nearly every facet of political life. It matters when it comes to assigning blame for the problems the country faces, and it sets up the lens through which political news events are filtered and stored in memory (Zaller 1992).

In previous decades, when our politics involved lower levels of polarization and the greater presence of cross-cutting social identities, it might have made sense for candidates to appear moderate on policy. They might take a popular position on a particular issue in the hope of peeling off moderate or cross-pressured voters from the opposing party, yet they had to be careful not to shift too far to the middle for fear of losing others or depressing the vote among their co-partisans. In recent years, however, the very meaning of ideology has changed, with the word "conservative" gaining meaning as a proxy for loyalty to Trump regardless of the policy preferences of the politician (Hopkins and Noel 2022).

If a person is a Democrat, however, not due to her policy preferences but because partisanship is a stable social identity reinforced by other overlapping identities, she is unlikely to be persuaded by a token attempt of a Republican to moderate on an issue in order to win her vote. Conversely if a Republican chooses his partisanship because the features of his identity also align well with the Republican Party coalition, no attempt by a Democratic candidate for elected office is likely to change his vote. The deep partisan divisions that run along social, racial, and class fault lines in the United States make it hard for the two sides to cooperate effectively (Mason 2015, Hetherington 2001).

In this kind of environment, it behooves candidates to (1) keep their primary electorate happy, (2) turn out co-partisans through campaign mobilization, and (3) convince the crucial middle ground of America that they are the best to represent those voters' needs. How can a candidate satisfy all three of those goals? The answer is unlikely found in staking out positions on important issues, as independent voters are not only less likely to vote but those who do vote are generally less knowledgeable about politics as well (Converse [1964] 2006; Delli Carpini and Keeter 1996). Instead, candidate character can provide an important signal to low-information voters about who will best represent their needs. As Popkin notes, American voters "want to hire competent people, but without the time or resources to evaluate their past performance, we must make a judgment based largely on clues to personal character" (1994, 65). Perceptions of compassion provide important cues to all voters, but it stands to reason that this cue should be especially influential when the partisan lens is not active. This could be in the case of pure independents (i.e., those who do not "lean" toward one party or another) or in the case of partisan primary voters.

Perceptions of compassion give voters a way to arrive at what they feel is an acceptable decision. This should provide candidates perceived as relatively more compassionate with a major advantage regardless of policy positions. While using these heuristic strategies is no guarantee that Americans will arrive at the "correct" voting decision (however one conceptualizes that), these strategies are nonetheless employed by a significant number of American voters. Because independents are lower information voters without strong ideologies or partisan stances on important issues, they will instead lean on their perception of candidate compassion. They will seek out a candidate who they believe "cares about people like them" and intuitively understands their needs. In that way, they believe that no matter how abstract or uninteresting an issue may be, the politician will look out for their interests.

As I have noted, much of this theory also applies to partisans in primary elections. While partisans are normally more knowledgeable about policy issues than nonpartisans, primary elections often present voters with competing choices that do not differ greatly when it comes to policy. As a result, the distinction between candidates in primaries is often on personality. The 2016 Democratic primary, for example, was largely portrayed as a contrast in style and not substance. In early 2015, Democratic strategist Hank Sheinkopf said Bernie Sanders was "the populist symbol," in strong contrast to Hillary Clinton's "establishment candidate" persona.[4] Sanders sought to portray Clinton as being out of touch, more interested in fundraising than in representing the views of normal Americans. I seek in this chapter to show not only that perceptions of compassion exert independent influence on voting decisions, but also that they are especially important in situations where the partisan lens is not active. This line of reasoning leads to the first set of testable hypotheses.

H1a: Compassion→Voter Choice Hypothesis: Believing a candidate for office "cares about people like you" will increase support for that candidate, even after considering the numerous other factors that influence voter choice.

H1b: Partisan Lens Hypothesis: Believing a candidate for office "cares about people like you" will be a stronger determinant of support in situations where the partisan cues are not accessible heuristics (i.e., pure independents and primary voters).

2.4 Who Cares? Let's Ask Voters

To provide initial evidence in support of these hypotheses, I look at those factors regular Americans name when asked to explain their vote. While self-reports on their own may not be compelling evidence that a character trait matters,[5] they at least provide some insight into those factors Americans *think* drive their voting decisions.

From election to election, polling companies update their questions to make the results more topical and interesting to a broad range of readers. This can make identifying the relative importance of compassion from year to year difficult. Yet in looking at polling data from the last 10 years, what becomes evident is that both pollsters and the voters seem to think compassion matters in voting decisions. Across different electoral contexts, pollsters

---

[4] "Socialist Sanders threatens Clinton more than made-for-TV O'Malley," *Politico*, May 28, 2015.
[5] Brendan Nyhan, "Why did I vote that way? Don't ask me," *New York Times*, November 4, 2014.

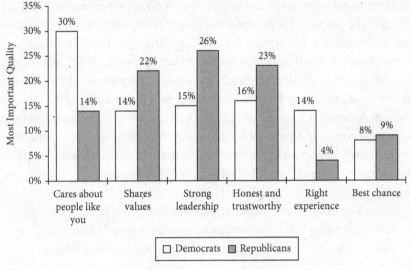

Figure 2.1 2016 Poll of Primary Voters—Most Important Quality in a Candidate

Source: Quinnipiac Poll, February 2016

frequently use a question featuring some variation of the description "cares about people like you" to gauge how strongly voters desire a politician who is in touch with their needs. Democrats, in particular, are likely to cite this type of "caring" as one of the more important qualities in a politician.

Figures 2.1 and 2.2 show the results from two different surveys (one from Quinnipiac and one from the Pew Research Center) that asked primary voters in 2016 and 2008 to name the most important quality in a presidential nominee. I examine these two elections because they are the two most recent elections in which neither an incumbent president nor a vice president was running, making both of the nominating processes fairly open, competitive, and not centered exclusively on the traits or attributes of the incumbent president.

The precise options offered to survey respondents differ between the two polls. "Can bring change," which was the most popular selection in 2008, was not even included in the 2016 poll. Yet even with these differences, we see that Democrats are overwhelmingly more likely to select "cares about people" when compared to Republicans. In 2016, 30% of Democrats selected "cares" compared to only 14% of Republicans. "Leadership," a trait owned by the Republicans (Hayes 2005), is the more common choice for Republican

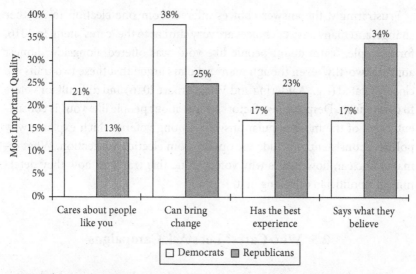

Figure 2.2 2008 Poll of Primary Voters—Most Important Quality in a Candidate

Source: Pew Research Center, January 2008

primary voters. The differences along party lines are important to note because, as I show later on in this chapter, Democratic candidates for the presidency generally have an advantage when it comes to perceptions of compassion. Even Democratic candidates we view as being relatively out of touch or insincere (e.g., Al Gore, John Kerry, Hillary Clinton) held an advantage in terms of compassion. In the case of failed Democratic candidates, it is not that they were seen as less empathetic than their Republican opponent, simply that they did not have the same degree of an advantage as more successful Democrats.

The 2008 poll from the Pew Research Center provides the most interesting results when considering the importance Democrats place on compassion. In 2008, "change" became the buzzword of the year. Barack Obama emphasized the concept of change in every speech, and his campaign rallies featured large blue signs with the word "change" written across them. As a result, it is not surprising to see that "can bring change" was the most popular choice among Democrats (and even the second-most popular among Republicans). Yet even in an election in which change was the primary message to Democratic voters, Democrats were still more likely to say that compassion was the most important quality in a candidate. 21% of Democrats selected "cares about people like you" compared to only 13% among Republicans.

Frustratingly, the answer choices offered from one election to another change, and many answer choices are very similar to the "cares" item. In 2016, for example, "cares about people like you" was offered alongside "honest and trustworthy," even though many scholars argue that these two traits are closely related (e.g., Aaldering and Vliegenthart 2016) and difficult for voters to distinguish. Despite these factors, "cares about people like you" is consistently one of the more popular answers among voters, which explains why pollsters consistently include the option from election to election. What remains unclear, however, is why voters value this trait and how they determine if a politician is lacking in it.

2.5 Who Cares? Let's Ask Campaigns

In addition to asking voters what attributes they value most in a leader, it is also useful to ask those who work on campaigns what messaging strategies they believe win over voters. To that end, I conducted a series of interviews with current and former campaign staff with experience working for both Democratic and Republican candidates. In these interviews, it was evident that issues of "character" are central to the messaging strategies employed by campaigns. Campaigns seek to connect with voters by presenting simplified messages that meld the personal characteristics of their candidate with the policies that the candidate champions. Yet these discussions also revealed that there is some awareness by the campaigns of "trait ownership." Because Democrats are viewed broadly as the more compassionate of the two parties, Democratic campaign operatives tend to put a special emphasis on this trait while Republicans talk about it more in the context of melding personality with policy.

Chris Myers, the former research director for the National Republican Congressional Committee (NRCC) characterized good campaigns as "one-trick ponies," focusing on the individual trait or issue that is likely to win a race:

> When people go to the ballot box, they just have so little room in their brains to store the different compartments of information. They have a predilection based on party, maybe some other attributes like gender or race or background or the way they talk or the job that they held, but generally speaking, it's just going to be a few characteristics that are the real driver.

Campaigns that simplify the choice for voters and repeatedly call up their one or two winning characteristics, Myers reasoned, are usually the most successful. The crucial aspect of campaigns, as he put it, was to simplify the choices voters had to make and "push those same buttons over and over again." By focusing on a small handful of issues and a single trait, campaigns could more effectively shape the perceptions of voters.

Jimmy Donofrio, a veteran of the Democratic National Committee (DNC) research department and the digital director for a number of independent political groups, also spoke of the need to simplify the choice for voters. Yet for him, the story more straightforwardly involved convincing voters that your candidate is *the* compassionate choice who can be trusted. "The thing people want to know is that you're going to take care of them. . . . That's a big part of the messaging. Figuring out how to present yourself as *like* the people who you want to vote for you." Donofrio noted that campaigns have many tools at their disposal for this messaging strategy, but campaigns must be skilled at employing them to avoid any messages backfiring.

Even those campaign operatives who do not identify compassion explicitly often allude to basic themes of personal credibility on feeling someone else's pain. A veteran of multiple Democratic presidential elections (who wished to remain anonymous) pointed out that

> a lot of people are trying to deal with an economy that's not really working for them, so making promises of change, especially changing Washington—everyone thinks that Washington is broken—so if you can give the impression that you're going to do something about it, they will probably support you.

Yet, as this operative noted, there are limits to messaging that campaigns can't address. The attacks on Mitt Romney's tenure at the private equity firm Bain Capital, she claimed, "were effective because they were sort of true." She continued:

> You can't just paint someone as something without there being any evidence. So, with Romney, he had his career at Bain where he was leveraging companies, workers got laid off, jobs were shipped overseas, etc. etc. But then on the campaign trail, he would give examples of [his heartlessness]. One of his first events even before he was actually running for president in 2012, he was in Florida at a coffee shop. He was hanging out with

unemployed people to talk about the economy and things like that, and he
starts with, "I'm also unemployed."

When asked how she would rate the Clinton team's performance messaging
around Hillary Clinton's personal character, she admitted that, although she
liked Clinton, similar problems existed: "Hillary Clinton was a well-qualified
person, but you can't just become charismatic because a consultant wants
you to."

Drawing from Hayes's (2005) theory of trait ownership, I have argued
that compassion will play a bigger role in the messaging strategies of
Democratic politicians. To better assess whether partisanship shapes campaign messages, I turn to the Presidential Primary Communication Corpus
(Scott 2021), which includes all major presidential speeches given by major-
party candidates from 2000 to 2020 ($N=3,364$). I apply the language inquiry
and word count (LIWC) dictionary developed by Graham, Haidt, and Nosek
(2009) to identify the different dimensions found in moral foundations
theory (MFT). This involves counting the number of words that appear in
a speech that fit with a particular topic with the dictionary developed ahead
of time to accurately assess the amount of language devoted to that topic.
Although the moral foundations literature is distinct from the candidate
character literature, some have argued that candidate character should be
interpreted through the lens of moral foundations theory (Clifford 2018).
Importantly, one dimension of MFT identified by scholars is the care/harm
dimension, while others include fairness, loyalty/in-group, authority/re-
spect, and sanctity/purity (Haidt and Joseph 2004). The care/harm dimension fits closely with the notion of compassion and empathy, making it a
suitable method for measuring compassion-related language in campaign
speeches.

In prior research, Neiman et al. (2016) found few differences between
Democrats and Republicans in their overall usage of language fitting the
care/harm dimension of MFT (though they did find Democrats were more
likely to use nurturant/caregiving language). Yet that research looked at
politicians across a host of activities involving governing, legislating, and
campaigning in both scripted and unscripted settings. Here, I focus exclusively on politicians for national office in their role as campaigners
in a scripted setting. Thus, the data are suitable to assess the degree to
which Democrats emphasize the role of compassion in their campaign
communications.

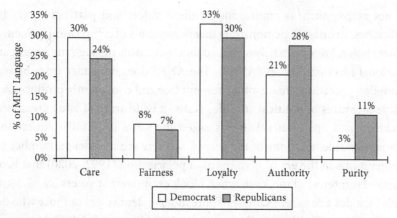

Figure 2.3 Proportion of Moral Foundations Language Devoted to Care, Fairness, Loyalty, Authority, and Purity (by partisanship of candidate)
Source: Presidential Communication Corpus (Scott 2021)

For ease of interpretation and to directly test the assertion that Democrats uniquely favor messages of compassion relative to messages involving some other dimension of candidate character, I look at the percentage of all MFT language devoted to care (Figure 2.3).

Democrats running for president use language related to care and harm more often. Across all five dimensions, Democrats devote roughly 6 percentage points more of their language to messages involving care or harm. Republicans, conversely, are much more likely to discuss matters related to authority, which follows Hayes's (2005) claim that the Republican Party owns traits related to leadership, as well as purity, a trait more closely associated with conservatism (Graham, Haidt, and Nosek 2009).[6]

2.6 Compassion in Presidential Elections: 1992–2020

With this chapter, I seek to show not only that compassion matters to voters, but also that it matters a great deal in situations in which the partisan lens

---

[6] The analyses here do not account for the fact that some candidates gave numerous speeches. Running these analyses using candidate-level fixed effects do not significantly change the findings presented here (those analyses are located in the appendix to this chapter). The estimated difference between Democrats and Republicans on the dimension of care increases from 6 points to nearly 12 and is statistically distinguishable from zero.

is not active, such as among independent voters and partisan voters in primaries. In order to demonstrate that perceptions of compassion influence voter choice, I rely primarily on data publicly available through the American National Election Studies (ANES). The ANES does not suffer from biased sampling procedures many other surveys face and consistently produces reliable measures of political attitudes across a wide array of issue areas (see Jackman and Spahn 2014). It has asked the same (or similar) questions across multiple iterations of the survey, so there are a sufficient number of observations in the era of high partisan polarization (1992–2020) that is of particular interest to me, even when I look exclusively at voters ($N = 7,388$). This includes a sufficient sample of pure independent voters or those who do not "lean" toward either the Democrats or Republicans ($N=1,465$). I focus on the following survey item: "How well does the phrase, '[he/she] really cares about people like you,' describe [politician's name]" (see appendix for greater detail). Unlike the Quinnipiac and Pew Research Center surveys examined earlier in this chapter, respondents are not forced to choose the most important trait. They are asked to rate the intensity with which the phrase describes a particular candidate. This is more useful than a binary measure since I seek to determine the degree to which variation on perceptions of compassion influence voter choice.

Because choosing a candidate on a ballot is a comparative exercise, ratings of candidate compassion in a vacuum are not particularly informative. Instead, I compare perceptions of compassion *in relation to* the opposing candidate. Therefore, I rely on the "Democratic compassion advantage" variable I described in Chapter 1, which simply subtracts the rating given to the Republican presidential candidate from the rating given to the Democratic candidate (resulting in a measure that goes from −4 to 4).[7] On this scale, a rating of −4 indicates that the respondent gave the highest evaluations of compassion to the Republican and the lowest evaluations of compassion to the Democrat. A rating of 4 would indicate the opposite, while a rating of 0 would mean that the respondent views the Democratic and Republican nominees for president to be equally compassionate.

---

[7] In 2008, the ANES changed the answer choices from a 4-point scale to a 5-point scale that included the middle category (3) "moderately well." To maintain comparability, I coded the 5-point scale as described above and the 4-point scale without a value for the number 3. This coding decision is consistent with analyses used by other scholars working in the field of candidate character traits (e.g., Holian and Prysby 2015).

Before looking at how compassion affects voter choice, I first establish that perceptions of compassion are not entirely endogenous to partisanship. Indeed, this research would be less important if Republicans and Democrats *always* saw their party's candidate as overwhelmingly more compassionate. I maintain that a large degree of variation on measures of caring cannot be explained by partisanship and global evaluations alone. The personal backgrounds of the candidates, the emotions they evoke, and other salient identities they share with the voters should also matter when it comes to determining whether a politician is compassionate.

Figure 2.4 shows the distribution of all ANES respondents from 1992 to 2020 on the Democratic compassion advantage measure. The results here reveal a surprising degree of variation. Democrats are motivated to see their candidate for the presidency as more compassionate, and Republicans on average do the same for their preferred candidate, but this relationship is far from deterministic. In fact, the modal value for responses among Republicans is to find no difference between the candidates, and nearly 13% of Republicans rated the Democratic candidate as more compassionate. Again, given the amount of time Democratic candidates talk about compassion relative to other character traits, this skew is to be expected. Yet even among Democrats, who on average view their candidate as far more compassionate, over 22% of them still saw the Republican as more or equally caring for people like them. The crucial bloc of political independents is the most

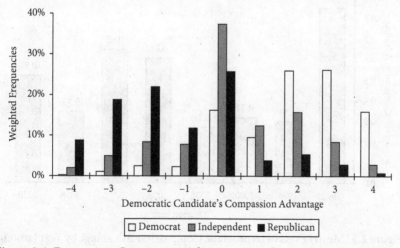

Figure 2.4 Democratic Compassion Advantage Distribution by Partisanship
Source: American National Election Studies, 1992–2020

evenly divided on which party's candidate is more compassionate, which
further lends credence to the argument that compassion could be especially
consequential among this voting bloc.

Figure 2.5 displays the extent of the advantage Democrats normally have
with regard to perceptions of compassion. Although Democrats in every
election since 1992 have had an advantage, there is a clear trend in which
the most successful Democratic candidates have been perceived as especially
compassionate. The 1992 election featured a Democrat in Bill Clinton whose
style contrasted strongly with George H. W. Bush, who critics described as
out of touch. Bush did not help himself on matters of relatability and compassion. Multiple instances over the course of the campaign, such as when
Bush appeared to be astounded by common grocery store technology and
when he checked his watch during a townhall presidential debate as a voter
asked a question, suggested he was not particularly connected or concerned
with the lives of normal people. The elder Bush's son, George W. (i.e., the
"compassionate conservative"), did much better. Though voters did not
perceive George W. Bush as more compassionate than either Al Gore or
John Kerry, his folksy style, contrasted against the more wooden figures of
Gore and Kerry, narrowed the gap. And while many might have expected
Donald Trump to be perceived as relatively out of touch (which is somewhat

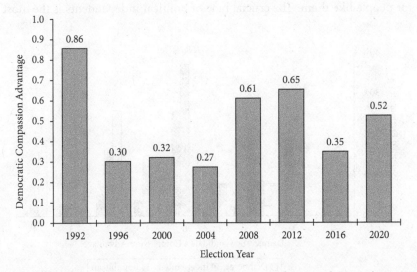

Figure 2.5 Mean Levels of Democratic Compassion Advantage by Year (among
voters)

Source: American National Election Studies, 1992–2020

true, according to the data), he did not perform all that much worse than Hillary Clinton. The gap of 0.35 in 2016 is similar to those of 2000 and 2004, elections in which a Republican was also successful. Only 1996 runs somewhat counter to this trend, as Bill Clinton's re-election was still successful despite not having the same compassion advantage it had in 1992.

Many factors determine election outcomes, but these descriptive statistics all show a common theme: politicians get more votes when they are perceived as more compassionate. Although Democrats are advantaged when it comes to the question of who cares more, Republicans who minimize the damage of this characteristic are more often successful in winning the presidency. Figure 2.6 shows respondents' reported voter choice across particular values of the Democratic compassion advantage, separated by party. Again, the trends we would expect to see hold true. Democrats in general are more likely to vote for the Democrat, but those few Democrats who do not see the Democratic candidate as more compassionate are unlikely to vote with their party in a general election. Republicans, likewise, are willing to vote for the Democrat if they see that candidate as more compassionate.

Figure 2.6 demonstrates two important features of American presidential elections. First, partisanship matters a lot. Even after we account for perceptions of compassion, the gaps in the three lines show clearly that partisanship impacts voter choice. Even among those Republicans who claimed

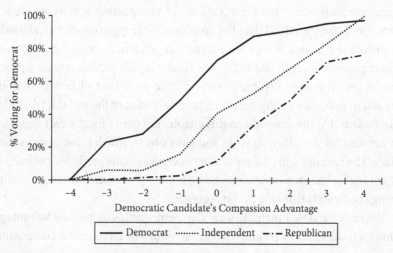

Figure 2.6 Voter Choice by Democratic Advantage on Compassion, Grouped by Partisanship

Source: American National Election Studies, 1992–2020

the two candidates were equally compassionate, we see that only 12% voted for the Democrat. Among Democrats who viewed the two candidates as equally compassionate, more than 70% voted for the Democrat. That all three lines have clear positive trends, however, should force us to consider the independent effect these individual evaluations of compassion have on voter choice.

The preferences of independent voters are especially interesting. When independent voters view the two candidates as equally compassionate, only about 40% of them vote for the Democratic candidate. Again, this reflects the fact that Democrats on average are perceived as more compassionate than their Republican opponents. If the Democrat is not perceived as doing better on compassion, a trait the Democrats own, independents are not particularly supportive. Yet when the Democrat is perceived as just 1 scale-point better than the Republican on perceptions of compassion, support for the Democrat surges to 53%.

These findings reflect the reality that partisanship alone does not explain perceptions of compassion. While partisanship helps explain why some voters will view one politician more favorably than the other, a significant portion of the electorate is willing to view the candidate from the opposing party as equally compassionate and sometimes *more* compassionate. And these perceptions have a profound impact on electoral fortunes.

The prior analyses have not accounted for the multitude of factors that simultaneously affect both perceptions of compassion and voter choice. I therefore use the ANES data but employ a more rigorous statistical model to make the case that voter choice is truly dependent on how compassionate voters perceive a candidate to be. The results in this section rely on a probit model that regresses two-party voter choice on a host of factors that are known to influence voting decisions (a full account of the variables included can be found in the appendix to this chapter). It uses a fixed-effect approach to account for the differing years and elections in which these surveys took place. The bars in Figure 2.7 represent the change in the predicted probability of voting for the Democratic candidate among partisans and independents, using coefficients from the probit regression.[8]

The only variable I manipulate is the Democratic compassion advantage. This method requires picking particular values of Democratic compassion

---

[8] Because omitted variable bias in a model predicting voter choice poses a major threat to the validity of the results, a large number of control variables are included here. These include perceptions of politicians' abilities as leaders, partisanship, considerations of retrospective personal finances,

advantage to compute what impact it has on voting for the Democratic candidate for the presidency. Because it is hard to imagine that any voter would move from one end of the scale to the opposite side, I choose not to examine extreme values in this analysis. Instead, I use the distribution of responses in the sample to guide my simulations. I therefore find the predicted probabilities of voting for the Democratic presidential candidate for individuals one standard deviation below and above the mean in terms of the Democratic compassion advantage variable. I furthermore examine predicted probabilities at observed values rather than average values, because observed values demonstrate the average effect of the treatment across all respondents in our sample. Examining the treatment effect for only the "average case" rather than for all observations is an inefficient use of data and narrows the scope of inference we can draw (Hanmer and Kalkan, 2013). Figure 2.7 represents a summary of these analyses. It demonstrates that, even when we control for the myriad factors known to influence public approval and voting decisions, the effect of compassion on voter choice is strong and potentially decisive.

The results show that not only do perceptions of compassion influence voter choice but also that this effect can be pivotal for voters in presidential elections. For the full sample, the effect is a massive 25 percentage points. Not only is this effect substantively large, but it is driven by voters who are of critical importance to winning the election. Democratic and Republican voters are fairly locked into their preferences. A Democrat on the low end of the Democratic compassion advantage scale would still be 87% likely to vote for the Democrat. Republicans on the high end of the scale would still only be 13% likely to support the Democrat. This reaffirms what political scientists have long claimed: partisanship matters. Yet even among these partisans, we still see an impact for compassion on voter choice to the tune of roughly 10 percentage points. These changes are still significant and would be decisive in any recent presidential election, so it is important not to discount the potential for compassion to influence the voting choices of even strong partisans.

. For independents, however, the effects are far more impressive. The effect of seeing the Democratic candidate as somewhat more compassionate than the Republican takes them from being only 25% likely to support the

considerations of prospective personal finances, considerations of retrospective national economic performance, considerations of prospective national economic performance, gender, ideology, age, race, education, and family income. Full regression outputs can be found in the appendix to this chapter.

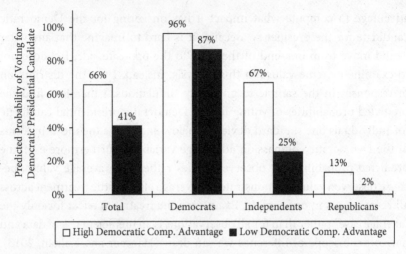

Figure 2.7 Predicted Probability of Voting for Democrat by Partisanship at Differing Levels of Democratic Compassion Advantage

Source: American National Election Studies, 1992–2020. Low and high Democratic compassion advantages are calculated by moving one standard deviation below the mean to one standard deviation above the mean in terms of this measure of advantage. This is done separately for each subgroup. For example, the marginal impact of compassion on voter choice for Democrats is calculated by moving from 0.4 to 3.6 on the measure of Democratic compassion advantage. For Republicans, it is calculated by moving from –3.2 to 0.5. That way, the values being used are realistic for all varieties of partisans.

Democrat to 67% likely. Not only is this 42-percentage-point effect substantively large, but it importantly crosses the 50% threshold where Democrats can expect to win a majority of this critical voting bloc. Much has been made in recent years about the importance of winning over the small number of undecideds who still exist from election to election, rejecting partisan entrenchments. That these voters' perceptions of a candidate's compassion alter their support should be of great interest to campaigns seeking a winning strategy.

2.7 A Case Study: Impact of Compassion in the Maryland Democratic Senate Primary

Though presidential elections offer the richest source of data to test the importance of compassion in the political arena, the theory underpinning the importance of compassion in voter choice operates similarly across many contexts. Chiefly, perceptions of compassion should play an important role in primary elections. In a general election, many voters rely on their partisan affiliation to select a candidate, yet independents cannot do this. Similarly, partisan voters weighing two candidates that belong to the same party cannot simply fall back on partisanship to inform their vote. Instead, they must find some other factor that differentiates the two politicians.

Here I rely on a survey from the 2016 Maryland Senate primary. I use observational data obtained through the Washington Post-University of Maryland Poll,[9] which included questions related to both voter choice and perceptions of compassion in the competitive Democratic primary for an open Senate seat pitting Chris Van Hollen against Donna Edwards ($N=617$). This election is especially illustrative of the theory I test in the next chapter with regard to the importance of a common identity (such as race or gender) as a driver of perceptions of compassion. Not only did the candidates share a partisan affiliation, thus reducing the role of partisanship as a determinant of voter choice, but they also differed in terms of both race (Van Hollen was white while Edwards was Black) and gender (Van Hollen a man and Edwards a woman). I therefore explore not only how perceptions of compassion influence voter choice but also how race and gender played a role in determining who cares about people *like you*. The answer choice scale on measures of compassion in this survey ranged from 1 to 4 (1="Not well at all," 4="Extremely well") but were recoded to run from 0 to 1.

Consistent with the notion that salient identities shape perceptions of compassion, shared identities appeared to play a role in determining whether voters saw Van Hollen or Edwards as more compassionate (Figure 2.8). The evidence suggests that white Democrats do not differentiate greatly based on race, using the party cue rather than the racial cue in evaluating the politicians. The difference among whites was both small and statistically insignificant. In contrast, Black voters overwhelmingly saw Edwards as being more likely to care about people like them ($p<0.01$). Despite Van Hollen and Edwards being indistinguishable in terms of partisanship, race served as a salient identity through which Democratic voters in Maryland perceived the character of the candidates. It is not surprising,

[9] This survey was administered using the best tools for probability sampling. Data was collected by the firm Abt-SRBI, using random-digit dialing of landlines and cell phones. Interviews were conducted using live callers.

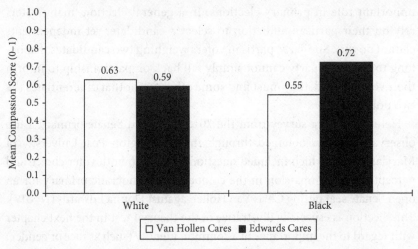

Figure 2.8 Perceived Levels of Compassion for Van Hollen and Edwards by Race
Source: Washington Post-University of Maryland Poll, April 2016

then, that Edwards is estimated to have won the Black vote by roughly 20 percentage points.[10]

Although not as drastic as race, gender may have played a minor role in the primary as well. Figure 2.9 shows that men gave Van Hollen and Edwards similar ratings in terms of compassion. Yet Edwards scored notably higher than Van Hollen among women. Was this simply the result of a shared identity or was this because Edwards had made her experience as a single mother a major selling point of her campaign? It is impossible for us to differentiate between these competing explanations due to the observational nature of the data, but these results are consistent with the claim that salient identities can shape perceptions of compassion. I explore this argument in the next chapter using an experimental design that controls for the potential confounders that threaten causal claims here.

Turning to the impact of perceptions of candidate compassion on voter choice, I find that these perceptions influence partisan primaries in much the same way as they influence presidential races. Using the same statistical

[10] Numbers reflect the results from exit polling data collected by Edison Media Research for National Election Pool, Washington Post, and other media organizations.

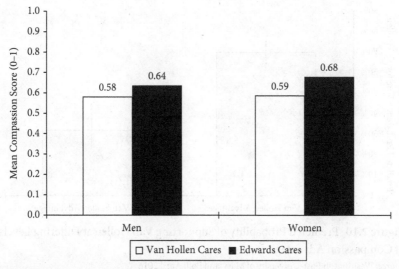

Figure 2.9 Perceived Levels of Compassion for Van Hollen and Edwards
by Gender
Source: Washington Post-University of Maryland Poll, April 2016

methods on the Maryland data as I used on the ANES, I generated predicted
probabilities for supporting Chris Van Hollen at one standard deviation
below the mean in terms of his advantage on compassion and one standard
deviation above the mean, holding all other variables in the model at
observed values.

The results here are clear. Van Hollen benefits greatly when he is perceived
as relatively more compassionate. Furthermore, the effect size we see in
these results, roughly 38 percentage points, is nearly equal to the effect size
found when looking at pure independents in presidential elections (Figure
2.10). Compared with the effect sizes found among partisans, which hovered
around 10 percentage points, the impact among independents and primary
voters is highly consequential. This underscores the importance of compassion for two reasons. First, independents often determine the outcomes
of elections. And second, the candidates that appear on the ballot in a general election most often get there by winning a primary. While many factors
undoubtedly play a role in who wins a primary, perceptions of compassion
play an absolutely critical role in determining the outcome of those elections
as well.

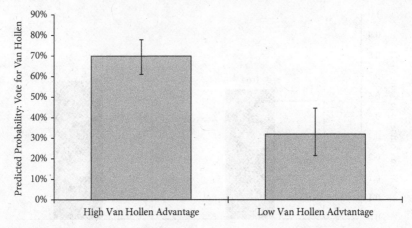

Figure 2.10 Predicted Probability of Supporting Van Hollen at Differing Levels of Compassion Advantage

Source: Washington Post-University of Maryland Poll, April 2016

2.8 Summary

In this chapter, I have argued that voters seek politicians who are compassionate because they believe that candidate can be trusted to look out for their best interests. Kinder (1986) notes that people seek to ascribe a motivation for the actions of politicians, which is made easier if they believe they understand what kind of person each leader is. Having positive perceptions toward a leader can make citizens find excuses when a politician they like fails, or it may make citizens give politicians credit for achieving things that might have been out of the politicians' control. Most voters do not have the time or energy to understand the intricacies of policymaking, nor is it reasonable for political scientists to demand that from them. As such, they fall back on their perceptions of whether a candidate is a good person who truly cares about people like them.

This chapter has sought to support two primary assertions about how compassion operates in the real world:

1. Campaigns are built in large part on the assumption that voters want a candidate who cares about people like them, with Democratic campaigns paying special attention to the trait of compassion. Voters are thus receiving messages that suggest they should be basing their voting decisions on the character traits of the candidates.

2. Voters reward candidates they perceive as caring, with effects especially
strong when the party cue is not an available heuristic.

The evidence supports these assertions. Discussions with campaign
professionals about what factors are key to successful campaigns invariably
mention the importance of convincing the public that the candidate is a good
and decent person who cares. And textual analyses of presidential primary
speeches show that language related to caring is used at a high rate, with
Democrats especially likely to rely on language related to caring or harm.

Analyses of surveys of American adults show that when voters believe
a politician cares about people like them, they are indeed more likely to
support them in an election, even after we control for the numerous other
factors known to influence voter choice. These effects matter across all party
categories but are found to be especially influential among independent
voters and partisan voters in primaries.

Using these observational analyses, I have also found evidence supporting
the theory that empathy can be conveyed through important commonalities
that serve to link the candidates to the voters. Candidates well-known for
talking on the campaign trail about their humble beginnings were often
perceived to be more compassionate. With regard to both race and gender,
voters appear to view the candidate who represents them descriptively as
being better able to relate to them. Yet observational analyses suffer from
limitations regarding causal inference. I therefore turn in the next chapter
to developing a theory of empathy through commonality, hypothesizing
that shared experiences, emotions, and identities serve as three key
commonalities that drive perceptions that a politician is truly caring. I then
support these hypotheses with a series of survey experiments.

Appendix

Analyses from Presidential Communication Corpus

Note: To assess the differences in use of moral foundations theory (MFT) language across partisanship, the parameters of ordinary least squares regression equations are estimated, regressing the percent of MFT words categorized as fitting the dimensions of caring, fairness, loyalty, authority, and sanctity on Republican partisanship. Because the candidates running for president appear multiple times in the data, observations are not independent of one another. I therefore cluster standard errors around the candidate.

Table A2.1 Ordinary Least Squares, Regressing Proportion of MFT Language on Each Dimension on Republican Partisanship (cluster standard errors in parentheses)

Variables	Caring	Fairness	Loyalty	Authority	Sanctity
Republican Partisanship	−0.051**	−00.014**	−00.034**	0.071**	0.028**
	(0.010)	(0.005)	(0.011)	(0.012)	(0.008)
Constant	0.296**	0.085**	0.331**	0.207**	0.081**
	(0.008)	(0.004)	(0.009)	(0.008)	(0.008)
Observations	3,364	3,364	3,364	3,364	3,364
Clusters	91	91	91	91	91

Note: Robust standard errors in parentheses.

**$p < 0.01$, two-tailed test

Items Used from ANES Data

Dependent Variable:

Voter Choice: Who did you vote for? [DEMOCRAT CANDIDATE/ REPUBLICAN CANDIDATE/SOMEONE ELSE]

Independent Variable:

Compassion Trait: Think about [DEMOCRATIC/REPUBLICAN CANDIDATE]. In your opinion, does the phrase "s/he REALLY CARES ABOUT PEOPLE LIKE YOU" describe [DEMOCRATIC/REPUBLICAN CANDIDATE] [EXTREMELY WELL, VERY WELL, MODERATELY WELL, SLIGHTLY WELL, or NOT WELL AT ALL/ NOT WELL AT

ALL, SLIGHTLY WELL, MODERATELY WELL, VERY WELL, or EXTREMELY WELL]?

Controls:

Leadership Trait: Think about [DEMOCRATIC/REPUBLICAN CANDIDATE]. In your opinion, does the phrase "s/he PROVIDES STRONG LEADERSHIP" describe [DEMOCRATIC/REPUBLICAN CANDIDATE] [EXTREMELY WELL, VERY WELL, MODERATELY WELL, SLIGHTLY WELL, or NOT WELL AT ALL/ NOT WELL AT ALL, SLIGHTLY WELL, MODERATELY WELL, VERY WELL, or EXTREMELY WELL]?

Retrospective Personal Finances: We are interested in how people are getting along financially these days. Would you say that [you/you and your family living here] are BETTER off or WORSE off than you were a year ago?

Prospective Personal Finances: Now looking ahead, do you think that a year from now [you/you and your family living here] will be BETTER OFF financially, WORSE OFF, or JUST ABOUT THE SAME as now?

Retrospective National Economy: Now thinking about the economy in the country as a whole, would you say that over the past year the nation's economy has GOTTEN BETTER, STAYED ABOUT THE SAME, or GOTTEN WORSE?

Prospective National Economy: What about the next 12 months? Do you expect the economy, in the country as a whole, to GET BETTER, STAY ABOUT THE SAME, or GET WORSE?

Partisanship: Generally speaking, do you usually think of yourself as a [DEMOCRAT, a REPUBLICAN/a REPUBLICAN, a DEMOCRAT], an INDEPENDENT, or what?

  Follow up: Would you call yourself a STRONG [Democrat/Republican] or a NOT VERY STRONG Democrat /Republican]? / Do you think of yourself as CLOSER to the Republican Party or to the Democratic party?

Ideology: Where would you place yourself on this scale [1–7, 1 EXTREMELY LIBERAL, 7 EXTREMELY CONSERVATIVE], or haven't you thought much about this?

Age: What is the month, day and year of your birth?

Gender: Male or Female

Race: What racial or ethnic group describes you?

Education: What is the highest level of school you have completed or the highest degree you have received?

Family Income: Information about income is very important to understand how people are doing financially these days. Your answers are confidential. Would you please give your best guess? The next question is about [the total income of all the members of your family living here/your total income] in 2011, before taxes. This figure should include income from all sources, including salaries, wages, pensions, Social Security, dividends, interest, and all other income. What was [the total income in 2011 of all your family members living here/your total income in 2011]?

Probit Models from ANES Data

Table A2.2 Probit Models, Regressing Vote for the Democratic Candidate on Perceptions of Candidate Compassion and Control Variables (standard errors in parentheses)

Variables	All	Democrats	Independents	Republicans
Dem. Compassion Advantage	0.303** (0.019)	0.260** (0.025)	0.409** (0.051)	0.350** (0.038)
Dem. Leadership Advantage	0.271** (0.018)	0.275** (0.027)	0.296** (0.049)	0.283** (0.030)
Retrospective Personal Finance	0.002 (0.026)	0.059+ (0.035)	−0.015 (0.067)	−0.057 (0.044)
Prospective Personal Finance	0.008 (0.034)	−0.025 (0.046)	0.095 (0.095)	0.019 (0.056)
Retrospective National Economy	0.087** (0.029)	0.075+ (0.043)	0.028 (0.077)	0.066 (0.045)
Prospective National Economy	0.012 (0.027)	−0.005 (0.036)	−0.036 (0.071)	0.072 (0.047)
Partisanship (7 point, 1=Democrat)	−0.279** (0.016)			
Ideology (7 point, 1= extremely liberal)	−0.212** (0.026)	−0.212** (0.036)	−0.167* (0.085)	−0.219** (0.041)
Gender (Male)	−0.021 (0.051)	0.003 (0.070)	−0.015 (0.135)	−0.043 (0.092)
Age	0.002 (0.002)	0.007** (0.002)	−0.005 (0.005)	−0.002 (0.003)
Race (white)	−0.266** (0.079)	−0.427** (0.111)	−0.227 (0.176)	−0.152 (0.153)
Race (Black)	0.300* (0.130)	0.175 (0.158)	0.584+ (0.321)	0.365 (0.282)

Table A2.2 Continued

Variables	All	Democrats	Independents	Republicans
Education	0.011	0.046	−0.083	−0.007
	(0.025)	(0.035)	(0.066)	(0.043)
Family Income	−0.007	−0.011	−0.034	0.001
	(0.010)	(0.015)	(0.026)	(0.018)
1992	−0.520**	−0.227⁺	−0.939**	−0.773**
	(0.097)	(0.156)	(0.258)	(0.152)
1996	−0.123	0.125	−0.786**	−0.217
	(0.110)	(0.156)	(0.295)	(0.159)
2000	−0.302⁺	0.074	−0.228	−1.265**
	(0.154)	(0.208)	(0.810)	(0.325)
2004	−0.060	0.217	−0.498	−0.358*
	(0.113)	(0.149)	(0.356)	(0.176)
2008	0.099	0.375*	0.124	−0.252
	(0.133)	(0.182)	(0.358)	(0.230)
2012	−0.350**	−0.059	−0.368	−0.688**
	(0.095)	(0.137)	(0.211)	(0.155)
2016	−0.179⁺	0.092	−0.091	−0.474**
	(0.098)	(0.134)	(0.217)	(0.158)
Constant	1.670**	1.055**	1.278*	0.610⁺
	(0.178)	(0.246)	(0.517)	(0.327)
Observations	12,648	6,576	970	5,102

Note: Robust standard errors in parentheses.
**$p<0.01$, * $p<0.05$, + $p<0.10$. ANES weights are applied

Items Used from 2016 Washington Post-UMD Poll

Dependent Variable:

Voter Choice: If the Democratic primary election for U.S. Senate in Maryland were held today and the candidates were (Donna Edwards) and (Chris Van Hollen), for whom would you vote?

Independent Variable:

Compassion Trait: In your opinion, how well does the phrase [s/he really cares about people like you] describe [Chris Van Hollen/Donna Edwards]?

1 Not well at all
2 Not too well
3 Pretty well
4 Extremely Well

Controls:

Effective Trait: In your opinion, how well does the phrase [s/he would be effective at getting things done as a Senator] describe [Chris Van Hollen/ Donna Edwards]?

1 Not well at all
2 Not too well
3 Pretty well
4 Extremely Well

Ideology: Would you say your views on most political matters are liberal, moderate, or conservative?

Gender: Pardon, but I'm required to verify—are you (male) or (female)?

Education: What was the last grade of school you completed?

1 8th grade or less
2 Some high school
3 Graduated high school
4 Some college
5 Graduated college
6 Post graduate

Family Income: Which of the following CATEGORIES best describes your total annual household income before taxes, from all sources?

1 Under 20 thousand dollars
2 20 to under 35 thousand
3 35 to under 50 thousand
4 50 to under 70 thousand
5 70 to under 100 thousand
6 100 thousand or more

Race: Are you of Hispanic origin or background?
(IF "YES," ASK:) Are you White Hispanic or Black Hispanic?
(IF "NO," ASK:) Are you white, black, or some other race?

1 White
2 Black
3 White Hispanic
4 Black Hispanic
5 Hispanic (no race given)

6 Asian

7 Other race

8 DK/No Opinion

9 NA/Refused

Age: What is your age?

Probit Model from Washington Post-UMD Data

Table A2.3 Probit Models, Regressing Vote for Van Hollen on Perceptions of Candidate Compassion and Control Variables (Standard Errors in Parentheses)

Independent Variable	Full Sample
Van Hollen Compassion Adv.	0.687**
	(0.172)
Van Hollen Effectiveness Adv.	0.849**
	(0.163)
Ideology (3 point, 1=liberal)	−0.039
	(0.136)
Gender (Male)	0.151
	(0.192)
Education (6 categories)	0.058
	(0.123)
Family Income	−0.029
	(0.069)
Race (white)	0.158
	(0.406)
Race (Black)	−0.465
	(0.421)
Age	0.002
	(0.006)
Constant	−0.004
	(0.006)
N	443

Note: Washington Post-UMD sampling weights applied.
**$p<0.01$

3

Empathy Through Commonality

3.1 The 2008 "Huckaboom" and a Theory of Political Compassion

When Mike Huckabee announced his intention to run for president in January 2007, few political pundits or power players within the GOP gave him any real chance of making noise in the primaries. As a relatively unknown governor of a southern state going up against the likes of well-known candidates like Rudy Giuliani, Mitt Romney, and John McCain, Huckabee struggled to gain name recognition and his fundraising suffered as a result. By the end of the first quarter of 2007, Huckabee had raised a paltry $544,000.[1] By February, some were pushing Huckabee to drop out and run for Senate, noting his failure to gain traction.[2] Even as late as the summer of 2007, Huckabee trailed well behind the leaders among the strongly conservative Iowa Republican electorate, polling at only 8%.[3]

Yet for all his disadvantages, early on some pundits noted qualities in Huckabee that gave him the chance to be an appealing dark-horse candidate. As the son of a mechanic, the first man in his family to graduate from high school, and a pastor in his community, Huckabee had a personal story that lent credibility to his folksy charm.[4] Pundits noticed that his personal style seemed to connect with voters. Even while Huckabee struggled to gain traction in early 2007, former Clinton adviser James Carville noted that, above all others in the 2008 field, Huckabee "likes people; he knows how to relate to people. He can talk the talk."[5] And while Democratic candidates looking back on eight years of George W. Bush as president could focus on the problems facing the country as a motivation for a change in leadership, Huckabee's

[1] "Republican Huckabee's hopes are Clintonesque, but treasury so far is not," *New York Times*, April 19, 2007.
[2] "Some push for Huckabee to run for Senate, not president," *The Hill*, February 28, 2007.
[3] Washington Post-ABC News Poll, "Iowa Republicans are not thrilled with presidential field," August 5, 2007.
[4] Michael Scherer, "Can Mike Huckabee out-charm the GOP big three?," *Salon*, March 5, 2007.
[5] James Carville interview by *Imus in the Morning*, MSNBC, February 27, 2007.

Feeling Their Pain. Jared McDonald, Oxford University Press. © Oxford University Press 2024.
DOI: 10.1093/oso/9780197696897.003.0003

jovial optimism fit the emotional sentiment of the Republican Party. As an evangelical Christian, Huckabee held the religious background of a crucial bloc within the Republican electorate, with more than a third of Republicans identifying with the evangelical movement.[6] Huckabee wowed in the GOP presidential debates with his defense of his Christian values and his quick, humorous wit ("What would Jesus do? Jesus was too smart to run for public office"[7]). Huckabee convinced conservative voters he could relate to them and understood their struggles. In August 2007, Huckabee scored a surprising second place finish in the Iowa Straw Poll,[8] and after another series of successful debates, Huckabee's popularity surged even further, culminating in a victory at the Iowa Caucuses.

What fueled this rise in popularity? Polls suggest that Huckabee's support was driven by the perception that he was compassionate, honest, and trustworthy. In July 2007, only 10% of GOP voters named him as the candidate who "best understands problems of people like you." By November, he was leading the field at 26%. The number viewing him as the most trustworthy similarly soared from 10 to 25%.[9]

Pundits attributed the "Huckaboom," to his easy-going nature and his ability to connect with voters. Despite their obvious ideological differences, comparisons to Bill Clinton, another Arkansas governor born in the town of Hope, were numerous. As the Washington Post described, "He's the affable, compassionate, good guy and rock-and-roll evangelical who plays guitar and wants to hang with the Rolling Stones."[10] These qualities were desirable to a large number of Republican voters. Ultimately, Huckabee's positive traits were not enough to win the nomination, as the dominant factor in the nomination contest shifted from questions of character to electability. Yet Huckabee's surge in the polls signaled the desire on the part of the electorate for a sincere candidate who could show he connected with the struggles of normal voters.

Stories similar to Huckabee's are found in nearly every campaign, where desirable personal qualities lead voters to evaluate a candidate more favorably.

---

[6] Ryan P. Burge, "The religious composition of the two major parties," Religion in Public, April 25, 2019.

[7] GOP debate, CNN, November 28, 2007.

[8] "Huckabee sees 'new life' in presidential bid after Iowa straw poll," Christian Science Monitor, August 17, 2007.

[9] "Huckabee gaining ground in Iowa," Washington Post, November 21, 2007.

[10] "Music to his ears; Mike Huckabee hit a chord in Iowa and is off and running," Washington Post, August 31, 2007.

Yet, in the minds of citizens, compassion in a politician is a means to an end, not the end itself. The end is good governance however the voter conceptualizes it, but it ultimately comes down to some instrumental or expressive benefit the voter believes she will receive for supporting the candidate she views as more compassionate. Any attempt to boil perceptions of compassion to a popularity contest where the voter sides with the candidate that is "more likable" ignores the mechanism through which voters arrive at that conclusion.

By ignoring the mechanism through which voters determine a politician is likable, scholars sometimes chalk up election outcomes to random chance. Achen and Bartels (2016) claim that "election outcomes are mostly just erratic reflections of the current balance of partisan loyalties . . . the choice between candidates is essentially a coin toss" (36). This may strike some as overstating the role of partisanship because it discounts other factors known to influence voter choice. Although partisanship is not the only influence on voter choice, the quote from Achen and Bartels reflects a pervasive way of thinking both in political science and in the public more broadly in this polarized era of American politics. From political scientist Brendan Nyhan's claim that "negative partisanship rules everything around me,"[11] to Alan Abramowitz and Steven Webster's claim in *Politico* that "negative partisanship explains everything," political observers could be forgiven for thinking there is little else that matters beyond polarization and out-group antipathy.

I do not discount the importance of partisan loyalties in voting decisions, nor do I contest Achen and Bartels' central argument that voters are ill-equipped at assigning blame and giving credit accurately. Yet the notion that tightly contested elections come down to a random coin toss ignores the tendency of voters to ultimately side with the candidate they see as more compassionate. This tendency, especially among politically unsophisticated citizens, may be prone to bias through poor information processing. It may result in "incorrect" voting decisions. Despite these problems, it remains a critical piece of the puzzle when examining voter choice and election outcomes (as I showed in the last chapter). Furthermore, the process through which voters determine whether a candidate is compassionate, I demonstrate, is not random; instead, it is the byproduct of key attributes possessed by the candidates and the voters themselves.

---

[11] Nyhan is also known for saying "partisanship is a helluva drug," which has been adopted by political commentators from Ezra Klein to Nate Silver.

For Mike Huckabee, Republican voters began to see the candidate's ability to empathize with their struggles as evidence he would do more than previous Republicans had to ameliorate the problems they faced. Though this method for evaluating a politician may or may not be normatively desirable (we cannot presume to know whether Huckabee's compassion for struggling Americans was genuine or not), I posit that it is a pervasive way of thinking in American elections that must be understood if it is to be addressed by political theorists and campaigns.

Compassion operates as a heuristic in much the same way as other types of cues. As Lupia (1994) notes, cues provided to relatively uninformed voters are heeded once the cue giver is deemed trustworthy and credible. I extend this theory by arguing that most voters are uninformed about policy minutiae and understand the need to delegate decision-making to trustworthy individuals who are not only competent but also understand the problems normal Americans face in their day-to-day lives. Voters view the compassionate candidate as the one who is better capable of this. If voters suspect a candidate is either (1) unaware of the problems everyday Americans face or (2) unmoved to action by these problems, why would a voter entrust them with elected office?

In examining this issue, the distinction between sympathy and empathy is paramount. A candidate who claims to care and wants to do something but is missing an empathetic connection may lack the motivation of someone who has firsthand experience with the problems others are facing. Any casual spectator in a campaign cycle will hear candidates wax poetic about the inspiring people they meet on the campaign trail and the stories they have heard. These messages help introduce candidates to voters in a positive way, but they do not convey an empathic connection. An empathetic candidate who understands what it's like to grow up poor and spent decades working with others in the community can recall personal experiences when talking to voters, making claims of caring more credible. Voters will view these politicians as being more likely to be moved to action once elected to public office than someone who is simply told by a random person on the campaign trail that there is a problem.

3.2 How Do Voters Conceptualize Compassion?
Empathy vs. Sympathy

In October 2016, Vice President Joe Biden said at a campaign event for Hillary Clinton that he was frequently asked whether he wished he could debate

Donald Trump. He told rally goers, "No, I wish I were in high school. I could take him behind the gym. That's what I wish."[12] For long-time observers of Joe Biden, the insinuation that he wanted to beat up Donald Trump for the things he said was not the least bit surprising. His sister Valerie, who had previously served as his campaign manager, noted, "the thing that Joe dislikes most in the world is a bully. And I think it has a lot to do with he knew what it was like to grow up being the brunt of a joke because he stuttered. I never even thought of it in terms of his struggling, he just went out and did it. But I think it's that empathy, which is different from sympathy."[13]

Valerie Biden Owens notes that her brother's ability to connect with people is rooted in his personal experiences, which convey empathy rather than sympathy. In the aftermath of Trump's 2016 victory, many in the Democratic Party believed that Biden was the best politician to take on the new president, precisely because of his unique ability to convey an authentic sense of empathy to the average American (a belief that found support in Biden's eventual victory over Trump in 2020). As part of the series of interviews I conducted for this book, I discussed the list of potential Democratic nominees prior to the 2020 primaries with former deputy research director for the Democratic National Committee and the Obama Re-Election Campaign Nick Hackworth. He summed up Biden's appeal this way:

> I think Biden is a great candidate. I think he's the perfect candidate against Trump. I think he's got the whole Scranton thing. This goes back to empathy. He's a Scranton guy, he can go to those white working-class places, and they actually like him. What I always liked about Biden was that the guy was vice president, a senator since he was thirty, but he still seems in awe of the coolness of a lot of the things about serving. He tears up when he's receiving the Presidential Medal of Freedom. You would think after that long in public service, he would be over it all, but he still has this authentic sense of wonder.

From quotes like these, it is clear that campaign professionals believe an authentic connection with voters, built through emotional and experiential commonalities, is key to winning support. Yet while many simply view

---

[12] "Biden suggests he wants to beat up Trump," *Politico*, October 21, 2016.
[13] *The Circus*, "Valerie Biden Owens speaks about her brother Joe's presidential aspirations," Showtime, October 31, 2016.

compassion in a candidate as an inherently desirable trait and, therefore, an end in itself, doing this hinders our ability to understand the underlying mechanism that connects perceptions of compassion with voter choice. Because of this, I not only demonstrate that these perceptions influence voting behavior but also seek to explain why some politicians are successful at cultivating positive perceptions of compassion while others are ridiculed as "aloof" or "out of touch."

Additionally, I differentiate between sympathy and empathy as sub-types of compassion in order to clarify what is going on in the mind of the voter. For the purposes of this work, "compassion" is broadly defined as caring about other people. The motives for this caring can be numerous, but voters can infer a motivation for caring so long as the candidate can convince voters she sincerely cares about average Americans, the issues that occupy their minds, and earnestly wants to make life better for people like them. A compassionate politician will be viewed as sympathetic or moved outwardly to help others. Yet, counterintuitively, empathetic messages should have a much stronger positive effect on perceptions of compassion than sympathetic messages. This is because voters are skeptical of vague claims of caring. Empathy, perceived through a commonality, overcomes this skepticism.

Holian and Prysby (2015) provide an in-depth examination of a number of different relevant candidate traits, paying special attention to empathy. Their definitions provide a useful point of departure for this work. Not only do the authors demonstrate the importance of believing a candidate "cares about people like you," but they also provide a working definition for empathy that helpfully encapsulates the way scholars have approached compassion in electoral politics. This definition, however, is problematic.

Holian and Prysby (2015) define empathy as "the recognition of another person's emotions, to feel what another person feels," yet they go on to say that "we can regard empathy as comprising compassion, concern, understanding, sympathy, and a general ability to feel what others feel, to walk in others' shoes" (29). While portions of this definition fit closely with the definition I use, they treat empathy as an umbrella term that encompasses compassion and caring. This is not unusual for scholars studying the factors that lead individuals to act in altruistic, pro-social ways. Yet for the purpose of studying perceptions of compassion in someone else, this definition poses a problem. This definition provides little insight into why voters want a candidate who has this trait. Empathy, for voters, is a means to an end, not the end itself. I argue that empathy is desirable because it suggests that a politician has, in her background, experiences that make her uniquely motivated and qualified to solve the problems many voters themselves face. Yet extant research does not examine how empathy leads to changes in political approval, leaving this mechanism unexplored.

As previously discussed, the importance of the distinction between sympathy and empathy comes down to differentiating between features of compassion that are inward versus outward looking. This means that I distinguish between what some call "empathic concern," which I define as sympathy, and "perspective taking" (Batson and Ahmad 2009; Batson, Early, and Salvarani 1997; Cuff et al. 2016; Underwood and Moore 1982), which I define as empathy. These may be semantic distinctions, but they are useful in explaining why some political messages are effective while others are not.

In psychology, "sympathy" (or empathic concern) is defined as the process through which someone becomes aware of another's affliction and recognizes it as something that should be alleviated (see, e.g., Mercer 1972; Nagel 1970; Zaki 2014). It is the "emotional response stemming from the apprehension or comprehension of another's emotional state or condition, which is not the same as what the other person is feeling (or is expected to feel) but consists of feelings of sorrow or concern for the other" (Eisenberg 2000, 671–672). Empathy is one way of spurring sympathetic behavior (Bernhardt and Singer 2012; Davis 2009), so an observer may use an empathetic connection as a heuristic or a shortcut in determining whether another has an intention of following through on sympathetic behavior. Yet one does not necessarily need to be empathetic to behave in sympathetic ways. Sympathy, then, is not about taking someone else's perspective or gaining a personal understanding as to *why* another is pained; instead, it is the awareness that another is experiencing a negative emotion that should be relieved.

Whereas sympathy is a heightened awareness for the pain of others, psychologists define empathy as an attempt on the part of one person to understand the subjective experiences of another (e.g., Wispé 1986). Sympathy refers only to a feeling of sorrow toward one who is suffering, but empathy refers to a more specific process of relating to another's pain. With empathy, there is a higher level of understanding for the specific experience. The empathetic actor is not only aware of the pain of another but also tries to understand the source of that pain as a way of knowing what that experience is like. As a result, an empathizer may be viewed as better able to relate to someone in pain than a sympathizer might. Sympathy and empathy, though closely related, are byproducts of different cognitive processes and, when those traits are perceived by voters, might force individuals to react differently to the candidates.

Unlike most research in psychology and neuroscience, the present goal is not to examine true feelings of empathy or sympathy, but rather perceptions of a candidate's character. Nearly all politicians will make claims of vague compassion, yet some will be more successful. Conveying empathy is key. Davis (1996) presents evidence that "judged empathy," or the belief that another person is empathetic, is linked to actual empathy (see also Dowell and Berman 2013). Studies of workplace environments show that empathy shares a close tie with effective leadership in organizational settings (Cooper and Sawaf 1997; Goleman 1998; Yukl 1998). Individuals who perceive leaders as empathetic, in turn, also view those leaders as more credible and trustworthy (George 2000; Lewis 2000). Kellett, Humphrey, and Sleeth (2002) identify empathy as one of two distinct pathways toward the perception that someone is a leader. It is a natural aspect of human behavior to judge whether someone has the ability to walk in your shoes, and there are reasons for voters to suspect that a politician who can do this will be more moved to help.

3.3 Empathy and the Sincerity Barrier

Given the space devoted here to distinguishing sympathy from empathy, it is worth noting why this distinction is so critical in the political arena. It matters because a skeptical electorate evaluating politicians will ask two questions: First, is this candidate aware of the problems I face in my day-to-day life? And second, do I believe this candidate when they say they care and will do something to solve those problems? With regard to the first question, either a candidate's sympathetic or empathetic appeal should be sufficient. Yet with regard to the second question about the sincerity of a candidate's message, a sympathetic appeal may not be as effective as an empathetic one.

In 1996, Bob Dole understood that Bill Clinton's ability to connect with voters was one of his greatest strengths. He therefore attempted to cast doubt on whether Clinton genuinely cared about struggling Americans. On the campaign trail, Dole attacked the Clinton administration for being a collection of Ivy League elitists. According to Dole, those who the Clinton administration had hired to work in the White House had "never sacrificed, never suffered." When given a chance to respond, however, Clinton made sure the attack backfired:

When Senator Dole made that remark about all the elitists, young elitists in the administration, one of the young men who works for me who grew up in a house trailer looked at me and said, "Mr. President, I know how you grew up. Who is he talking about?"[14]

Throughout the 1996 campaign, Bob Dole consistently pointed to policies or specific actions he had taken as evidence of his sympathetic nature. And although Dole was clear to make the connection between his legislative experience and his compassionate attitude toward others, those appeals were still sympathetic ones. Clinton, however, did not point to a legislative achievement to make his case, but to his personal history and to the stories of those who worked for him as evidence that the work they were doing in the White House was meant to better the lives of those less fortunate. This distinction is something voters pay attention to—and it makes a difference in who they will vote for.

Though politicians are not often viewed as particularly trustworthy individuals, those operating in today's highly polarized and toxic environment find additional hurdles in appealing to voters across the partisan spectrum. This trust to which I refer is not a generalized trust in human beings (i.e., people in general are good); rather, it is a self-interested trust that seeks to determine the likelihood that some politician will make good on her promises and deliver a better life to citizens (i.e., this person will be good to me).

If a voter does not trust the politician who claims to be compassionate without evoking some commonality with the voter to lend the claim credibility, it makes little sense for her to offer support. A sympathetic appeal may be sufficient to convince some voters, but it will likely fail for many more cynical citizens. I refer to this skepticism as the *sincerity barrier* in this research. While the sincerity barrier describes a cynicism likely felt by most voters evaluating campaign promises, levels of skepticism will vary from person to person in a given election.

The existence of the sincerity barrier explains the different roles sympathy and empathy play in cultivating positive perceptions of compassion. While empathy refers to a switch in viewpoint, to feel an emotion *as if* you were somebody else, sympathy refers to a feeling of sorrow for someone else's problems. Claims of sympathy from political candidates are common, though

---

[14] Transcript of the first televised debate between Clinton and Dole, October 7, 1996.

we often associate them with politicians who are not particularly effective at cultivating positive perceptions of compassion. In 2012, Mitt Romney employed the line, "I'm in this race because I care about Americans" when asked what motivated him to run for the presidency. This supposed motivation seemed like an apparent effort to overcome stories of his personal wealth and business experience, which often portrayed Romney as an unfeeling, wealthy businessman.[15] Yet Romney's claim to care did not necessarily mean he could put himself in someone else's shoes, so we cannot classify this as an empathetic appeal. Without a shared experience, identity, or emotion to connect Romney with the voters, claims of caring can be met with suspicion. As a result, concerns about Romney's sincerity persisted, and there remained a perceived disconnect between Romney and most American voters.

In summary, empathetic appeals should be especially effective when it comes to increasing positive perceptions of compassion for a political candidate. Sympathetic appeals should also be somewhat effective in improving these perceptions, as they at least represent an attempt on the part of the candidate to convey to voters that they are aware of the issues facing most Americans. Still, there remains a sincerity barrier that sympathetic appeals may not be able to overcome for a significant subset of more skeptical Americans. As a result, empathetic appeals should drive up positive perceptions of compassion more greatly than sympathetic ones.

3.4 Dimensions of Empathy

In studying the various ways psychologists have defined empathy and differentiated it from sympathy, it becomes clear that empathy in the individual operates as an extension of self. The empathizer can feel the emotions of another as if they were their own precisely because the line between the two individuals is blurred. Most people unconsciously engage in empathetic behavior, where the concept of self is extended to another, yet individuals are inconsistent when it comes to the particular circumstances under which they will engage in this sort of extension.

Empathy as an extension of self in modern society can be thought to operate as concentric circles, with those who are closer to you as being the easiest objects for empathy. Individuals feel stronger connections

---

[15] Mitt Romney interview by Soledad O'Brien, CNN, February 1, 2012.

to those in their families, to those in their communities, to those in their states, countries, regions, and so on (Nussbaum 1996; Slote 2001). Beyond this, there are ties based on cultural commonalities, such that people who belong to the same race or ethnicity may feel a deeper bond and be able to blur the line between self and other more easily (Dawson 1994). The greater the capacity for empathy, then, the easier it is for that individual to extend their conception of self beyond the racial, regional, and religious divisions that segment communities. Within the United States, traits such as race, religion, class, and sometimes region can influence the people with whom one identifies and for whom one can more easily empathize.

While these traits refer to an individual's ability to empathize with another, they also play a large role in how we perceive whether another will empathize with us. Will a middle-income Black woman believe to any degree that a wealthy white man cares at all about her? Will a farmer believe someone who works in academia understands their day-to-day struggles? Unlikely. These people share little in common in terms of identity or experiences, so their attitudes toward society and government are not likely to align. Whether we consciously think about it, we understand that particular salient identities shape our life experiences, which in turn shape our individual political attitudes and our feelings toward government.

It is precisely for this reason that I consider the manner in which we perceive empathy in others (namely candidates for public office) as somewhat more complicated than true empathy in ourselves. The better a candidate for public office can convince the voters that they reside in one of the closer concentric circles that define empathic capabilities, the easier it will be for them to win over those individuals' support.

In social psychology, scholars have identified what is known as the "similarity-attraction effect." This is the basic theory that suggests that people view favorably those they perceive to be like them in important ways (Byrne 1971; Holland 1959; Newcomb 1956). The types of similarity are numerous, though they have been said to include personality, attitudes, values, and physical attributes. Although the theory of similarity-attraction is not often discussed in terms of empathy, the theory I lay out here suggests that empathy may be one reason why we are attracted to those who are similar to ourselves. There are a number of signals Americans receive that suggest a candidate can, indeed, blur the line between themselves and the voter. These cues are transmitted through the politically relevant commonalities that exist to bind the candidate with the voter. Namely these include experience, emotion, and identity.

3.5 Experiential Empathy

Political empathy, as the literature in psychology notes, implies that the politician has the ability to experience whatever hardship the voter is experiencing *as if* it were her own. With experience, the connection from the politician to the voter should be relatively straightforward and go something like: "The American people are facing hardships, and I have handled hardship too. So I know what it's like to have personally lived the same types of experiences." With empathy of this type, intuitively one might expect that the personal backgrounds of the voter and politician should matter a great deal. Yet this is not always the case. As opposed to a working-class voter, a rich voter observing Mitt Romney's upper-class upbringing and successful business career likely viewed the candidate as truly caring about people like him. Yet this is not the classical conception of political compassion, nor is it the conception I use in this work to define experiential empathy. This is due to the fact that very few Americans believe themselves to be extremely wealthy or out of touch with the experiences of the middle class, so viewing a candidate as having those qualities should only appeal to a very narrow portion of the electorate. Everybody from political opponents to comedians to even those in the news media portrayed Romney as an "out-of-touch" candidate.[16] Romney, much like John Kerry or even George H.W. Bush, did not fit the classic "every man" image scholars find often characterize successful campaigns (Sullivan et al. 1990).

That is not to say that class is irrelevant in judgments about American politics. Indeed, Piston (2018) notes that attitudes toward the rich and poor explain a great deal about attitudes toward redistributive politics in the United States. Yet the "prototypical" American is neither wealthy nor poor, and individual wealth does not predict the degree to which Americans feel a strong attachment to their national identity (Theiss-Morse 2009, 49). In short, most Americans believe they reside somewhere in the middle class and believe the average American resides in that group as well. Appeals to "middle-class

---

[16] Amy Bingham, "Is Mitt Romney out of touch?," ABC News, February 27, 2012, http://abcnews.go.com/Politics/OTUS/mitt-romney-touch/story?id=15801839.

Americans" are ubiquitous in American politics and for good reason, since it represents one of the broadest appeals in campaign politics.

Being from a wealthy background, however, does not make it impossible for a candidate to successfully cultivate these perceptions. George W. Bush, for example, came from a wealthy political family, but because of his demeanor and the message he conveyed, Bush was not perceived as an out-of-touch East Coast elite. Bush portrayed himself as a rancher, somebody who could relate to people living in the rural areas, while simultaneously speaking Spanish to the growing Latino community in Texas and eventually nationwide. His personal style and reports of his checkered past seemed to make him more relatable. As *Newsweek* put it, "He went to Yale, but seem[ed] to have majored in beer drinking at the Deke House."[17] Bush was further juxtaposed in 2004 by John Kerry, a man of equal privilege, but one who *seemed* privileged. Bush was able to grab the mantle of the "common man" in 2004 despite lacking the same background as most Americans.

The reason Americans want an "every man" or "every woman" in elected office (Sullivan et al. 1990) likely stems from the fact that most voters view themselves as typical, everyday Americans. According to a 2015 Gallup poll, only 1% of Americans classified themselves as "upper class."[18] Numbers such as these reflect an anxiety felt by almost all Americans about their personal finances, an anxiety they feel the super-rich does not experience. Experiential-based empathy in politics normally manifests as economic hardship, though I do not rule out the possibility that there are other experiences that can serve as similar linkages to the voting public (I explore the experiential link of parenthood in the next chapter). Politicians with military histories, for example, often reference their time in the armed forces when conveying a sense of compassion for the sacrifices of military families. The reason I focus on economic hardship is that most Americans, even those relatively well-off, are worried about future financial security. If a candidate can convince voters that they understand at a personal level the kind of anxiety average Americans face, they appeal to a broad array of voters. If, however, that same candidate tried to appeal to individuals of a particular race or faith, they risk alienating a broad swath of the voting public that does not identify with that race or faith.

---

[17] Evan Thomas, Daniel Peterson, and Debra Rosenberg, "The Sons Also Rise," *Newsweek*, November 16, 1998.

[18] Gallup, "Fewer Americans identify as middle class in recent years," April 28, 2015.

Given the way Americans think of themselves and the anxieties they face, I posit that messages from politicians do not need to be specific to the circumstances voters themselves face but can instead reflect a shared experience that comes from worrying about future security and prosperity. While a farmer might react positively to a politician who is also a farmer, the alignment of such specific life experiences may be rare unless those rural experiences are especially common among the constituency the politician seeks to represent. Politicians are running to represent people with diverse backgrounds, so any theory that requires politicians to have experiences identical to those of the voter would be of limited value. The farmer, then, may not need to hear that a politician comes from a farming family in order to trust that the politician will deliver on her promises once in office. So long as she can convince the farmer that she understands the struggles that come with living that lifestyle, such as worrying about future income, planning for retirement, or saving for a child's education, she can cultivate positive perceptions of compassion. In this sense, a politician can make a personal connection with the voter without making the appeal overly specific. Experiential empathy, normally conveyed through personal stories of economic struggle, ends up being rather different than sympathy where there is no personal experience to fall back on.

Sympathetic appeals are still common. In the earlier example from Mitt Romney, he simply claimed to be running because he cared about people. This contrasted strongly with the style of his opponent, President Obama. In talking about the crush of student loan debt, Obama was able to make the claim that "I was in my 40s when we finished paying off our debt and we should have been saving for Malia and Sasha by that time."[19] The easiest way for Obama to make an empathetic appeal, as seen here, was to recall his personal experiences or those of his family. Having lived this personally provided him the background to understand the stress student debt puts on people in a way simply being aware of the problem would not. Mitt Romney, however, came from a wealthy family and his personal wealth was a talking point throughout much of the campaign. No matter how much Romney may have wanted to make an empathetic appeal on the issue of student loan debt, his ability to do so was limited.

The example of Romney helps explain why candidates do not always choose to employ empathetic appeals. While candidates undoubtedly

[19] *Chicago Sun-Times*, June 10, 2014.

pander to their audiences, pandering has limits when there is no common experience to fall back on. Hillary Clinton's 2016 candidacy encountered this problem when she appeared to have different messages to different audiences. As a politician in the public eye for decades, voters were well aware that she had not lived the typical American life. This already put her on shaky footing to appeal to working-class voters. When leaked transcripts revealed she claimed to support open borders when speaking to the financial industry,[20] it damaged her credibility with working-class voters about protecting American industries from cheap imports. As a result, Clinton was put in the difficult position of needing to convey sympathy while media reports undermined her capacity for empathy.

Ultimately, although sympathetic appeals may not be as effective as empathetic appeals due to suspicions of insincerity, they are better than making no claims of caring. While some voters may consider claims of sympathy dubious, these claims at the very least provide an answer to the question of whether a candidate is aware of the problems facing everyday Americans and understands that voters expect progress on these issues. The degree to which they are effective is critical for politicians who, like Romney, come from wealthy backgrounds and cannot claim to have had the shared experience of student loan debt or the multitude of other experiences voters may consider relevant when forming an impression of a candidate's capacity for compassion.

Taken together, these theoretical considerations lead to a testable hypothesis. When trying to convince a skeptical public that a politician truly cares about the average person, an empathetic appeal leveraging personal experiences should be more effective than a sympathetic appeal. That said, a sympathetic appeal still conveys to voters that the candidate is aware of some of the problems voters face, so they should be effective relative to no compassionate appeal. Stated formally:

H2a. Experiential Empathy→ Compassion Hypothesis: A politician who makes a credible empathetic appeal to voters relying on their personal experience will be perceived as more compassionate than a politician who makes a sympathetic appeal (which does not include a reference to personal experience), who in turn will be perceived as more compassionate than a politician who makes no appeal.

[20] *Politico*, October 19, 2016.

H2b. Sincerity Barrier Hypothesis: Skepticism in the general public will drive the differential effects between empathetic and sympathetic appeals.

Study 1—Experiential Empathy

To assess the importance of experiential empathy and test for the existence of the "sincerity barrier" facing politicians employing sympathetic appeals, I rely on a survey experiment administered in 2016 on a volunteer sample of 1,432 respondents[21] from Survey Sampling International (SSI).[22] The experiment portrays David Allen, a fictitious politician running for the U.S. House of Representatives, making either a sympathetic appeal, an empathetic appeal, or an appeal with no direct claims of compassion to voters.

The experiment was designed to isolate the mechanism central to the theory undergirding experiential empathy and the sincerity barrier. I use a fictitious politician but strive to provide enough detail to make him seem real. While the respondent is unfamiliar with David Allen, this lack of knowledge would not be unusual for a House candidate, especially for one early in the campaign cycle. Furthermore, this design limits any influence global evaluations of Allen could have on individual trait evaluations, since respondents have no prior knowledge about him. I manipulate both the message he conveys to supporters and his partisanship in order to examine the effect of having firsthand personal experience with hardship. Because some respondents will share Allen's partisanship and others will not, I can also examine whether empathetic messages more effectively overcome the sincerity barrier I suggest should be highest when the voter and the politician are not co-partisans.

The use of a fictional politician was necessary for two reasons. First, the primary goal of this research is to establish that voters, at least in the abstract, respond more favorably to a politician who makes an empathetic appeal rather than a sympathetic one. To do this, I prioritize experimental control

---

[21] This represents the total sample used after eliminating respondents who failed an attention check at the outset of the experiment.

[22] SSI (which has since been renamed Dynata) is a suitable platform to test these messages because, though the sampling technique was not purely random, SSI aims to be representative of the voting-age population in the United States. Scholars who have examined SSI samples find that their surveys yield highly accurate results that replicate the relationships found in surveys using probability-based sampling methods (e.g., Ansolabehere and Rivers 2013; Berinsky, Huber, and Lenz 2012). Analyses presented apply probability weights based on age, race, education, and income.

over ecological validity (McDonald 2020). Furthermore, placing the hypothetical candidate in the context of a congressional race, where name recognition is often low, minimizes the loss of external validity. Second, the use of a real politician would make it difficult to examine the role of the sincerity barrier, which is central to my theory. Because I operationalize this concept by examining whether the candidate and the respondent are co-partisans or out-partisans, I cannot use a real politician for whom partisanship is immovable. With these considerations in mind, I constructed the survey vignettes as follows:

Control: David Allen, a local grocery store owner, is running for a seat in the U.S. House of Representatives as a Democrat (Republican). He is forty-eight years old and has two children with his wife of twenty years. While he has long been a prominent citizen in his community and active in local politics, this is the first time he has run for Congress. In his first public speech since filing to run for office, Allen told the crowd, "I am asking each and every one of you for your vote this upcoming November election."

Sympathy: David Allen, a local grocery store owner, is running for a seat in the U.S. House of Representatives as a Democrat (Republican). He is forty-eight years old and has two children with his wife of twenty years. While he has long been a prominent citizen in his community and active in local politics, this is the first time he has run for Congress. In his first public speech since filing to run for office, Allen spoke of how much he cares about struggling families as his motivation for running. Allen told the crowd, "I care about the neighborhood mailmen and the part-time secretaries. I've heard the stories of grandfathers who worked as coal-miners to scratch out a living but couldn't even afford indoor plumbing. I've talked to families who have lived this hardship, and I care about those struggling to make ends meet. I'm running for Congress to help those Americans. I am asking each and every one of you for your vote this upcoming November election."

Empathy: David Allen, a local grocery store owner, is running for a seat in the U.S. House of Representatives as a Democrat (Republican). He is forty-eight years old and has two children with his wife of twenty years. While he has long been a prominent citizen in his community and active in local politics, this is the first time he has run for Congress. In his first public speech since filing to run for office, Allen spoke of his own history growing up in a struggling family as his motivation for running. Allen told the crowd, "My dad was the neighborhood mailman and my mom worked as a part-time secretary. My grandfather worked as a coal-miner to scratch out a living but couldn't even afford indoor plumbing. My family has lived this hardship, so I understand the struggles of those trying to make ends meet. I'm running for Congress to help those Americans. I am asking each and every one of you for your vote this upcoming November election."

Although Allen is a fictional candidate with a fabricated backstory, the message was modeled off real speeches given by John Kasich and Rick Perry during their failed presidential runs. Kasich routinely referred to his father, "John the Mailman," and his family's ties to coal country, while Perry discussed his childhood in Paint Creek, Texas, growing up without indoor plumbing.

The differences between the treatments are subtle yet important. In the sympathy treatment, David Allen invokes the people he has met on the campaign trail (as politicians often do) as his motivation for enacting positive change in office. Yet here there is nothing personal that should lead a voter to believe that he is especially motivated to solve the problems of everyday Americans. In the empathetic treatment, the mailman and the secretary are not abstractions he has learned about from the campaign trail but are instead central pieces of his family identity. For individuals approaching David Allen with suspicion, having blue-collar values "in his bloodstream" should be more convincing than simply claiming to have had contact with blue-collar Americans.

Respondents rated Allen in terms of perceptions of compassion. For this survey, I rely on a traditional measure used to gauge perceptions of compassion on the American National Election Studies (ANES), which asks respondents, "how well does the phrase 'he really cares about people like you' describe" the politician in question. For the purposes of the present research, that candidate was David Allen. Responses to this question as well as a measure of overall favorability were recorded on 5-point Likert scales. These scales are recoded from 0 to 1 so that differences between groups can be interpreted as the percentage point changes across the response scale.

Results
The experiential empathy → compassion hypothesis and the sincerity barrier hypothesis state that a candidate who makes a credible empathetic appeal

will be perceived as more compassionate than someone who makes a credible sympathetic appeal, and that this effect will be driven mostly by those for whom skepticism should be highest. On the one hand, empathetic appeals are made primarily by leveraging the personal experiences the politician has had or those of individuals close to them (such as close friends or family). Sympathetic appeals, on the other hand, occur when claims of caring are made without invoking any kind of personal connection to lend that claim authenticity and sincerity. It is for precisely this reason, suspicion about a lack of sincerity, that I argue the effects will be driven by those for whom skepticism is highest. I choose to operationalize skepticism in this section by looking at co-partisans (people who share David Allen's partisanship) and out-partisans (those who belong to the opposing party). This approach recognizes that one ramification of in-group and out-group dynamics is that trust and belief in the sincerity of a speaker should be higher among in-group members than out-group members.

I assess the impact of empathetic and sympathetic appeals by examining the mean differences between conditions for the 2016 SSI experiment. The results portrayed in Figures 3.1 and 3.2 represent the increase in perceptions of David Allen's capacity for compassion when respondents are treated to a sympathetic or empathetic message compared to the control.

Looking first at the impact sympathetic and empathetic appeals have on perceptions of compassion, I find that David Allen is, not surprisingly, perceived as substantially more compassionate when he makes some sort of compassionate appeal (Figure 3.1). Among co-partisans, even the sympathetic appeal modestly boosts positive perceptions of Allen's compassion by a statistically significant margin. Among out-partisans, the effect appears to be positive, though it is no longer statistically significant. Candidates who cannot make credible empathetic appeals, then, are well served by outwardly claiming to care about less fortunate individuals even if there is no personal or family history to lend credibility to that claim. Although these claims may not win over skeptics, they are still received warmly by those sharing the candidate's partisanship.

What is more interesting, however, is that the empathetic appeal significantly outperforms the sympathetic appeal, with the difference especially pronounced among out-partisans. The gap between the sympathetic and empathetic appeal more than doubles when looking only at those individuals who belong to the opposing party of David Allen. For context, out-partisans in the control condition give Allen an average rating of 0.42 (on a 0–1 scale)

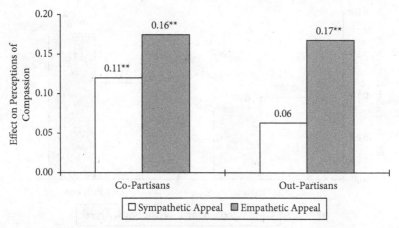

Figure 3.1 Effect of Sympathetic and Empathetic Appeals on Perceptions of Compassion Among Co-Partisans and Out-Partisans

**Effects are statistically significant at $p<0.01$

Note: Differences between the sympathetic appeal and empathetic appeal conditions are statistically significant for the total sample (at $p<0.05$) and among out-partisans (at $p<0.05$).

on compassion. For individuals in the sympathy condition, the number rises but stays below the 0.5 threshold. For out-partisans in the empathy condition, however, that number rises significantly to 0.59. While Allen is a fictional candidate without the baggage of many real politicians, the fact that individuals from the opposing party on average view him as truly caring about people like them is noteworthy. In a congressional campaign such as the one that is proposed in this experiment, a relatively unknown politician is realistic. This suggests that, when introducing a candidate to a polarized and skeptical American electorate, campaigns can make empathetic appeals that work across the partisan divide—they win over individuals belonging to the opposing party without alienating voters in their base. These data cannot speak to whether the more positive evaluations of the empathetic candidate will ultimately translate into greater vote shares, but the initial result is encouraging.

I also examine the possibility that sympathetic and empathetic appeals are strong enough to improve not only specific evaluations of compassion but also translate to overall favorability. As shown in Figure 3.2, the importance of the sincerity barrier becomes even stronger. While compassionate appeals *do* boost approval for David Allen, the difference between a sympathetic and empathetic appeal is far more muted when looking

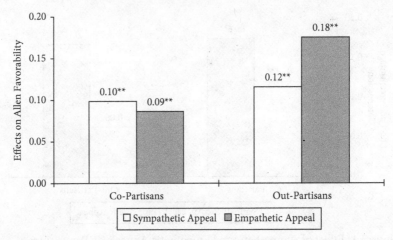

Figure 3.2 Effect of Sympathetic and Empathetic Appeals on Candidate
Favorability Among Co-Partisans and Out-Partisans
**Effects are statistically significant at $p<0.01$
Note: Differences between the sympathetic appeal and empathetic appeal conditions are only
statistically significant among out-partisans (at $p<0.05$).

exclusively at co-partisans. As I have argued, less skeptical individuals will
give their preferred candidate the benefit of the doubt and rely on partisanship to inform their overall evaluation of a politician. As a result, they
view him as similarly favorable even when he makes only a sympathetic
appeal rather than an empathetic one. Among out-partisans, however,
the story is much different. While those who share David Allen's partisanship do not support him at higher rates when the empathetic appeal is
made, those who belong to the opposing party view him in a significantly
more favorable light if he points to his personal experience as his motivation for caring. These results again reaffirm the importance of empathy
among those for whom skepticism is highest. The 6-point gap in overall
favorability is not only statistically significant, but it also substantively
meaningful in the broader context of electoral politics. Partisan voters
who view the opposition candidate in a more favorable light will feel more
ambivalent about the choices presented to them. Ambivalent voters see
the political world more clearly and therefore make more careful political choices (Lavine, Johnston, and Steenbergen 2012). In an age where
negative partisanship tends to drive so much of political behavior, these
results suggest there are ways of introducing more clear-thinking means
of selecting political leaders.

These findings present some normatively desirable implications. In particular, they suggest that the most effective messages are also the least polarizing. It is worth noting that out-partisans move more favorably for David Allen on both perceptions of compassion and overall favorability when he makes an empathetic appeal. This finding might strike some as odd at first. Individuals from the opposite party are the hardest to persuade, but here the impact of an empathetic appeal is at its greatest when the party of the citizen and politician do not align. Although I have noted that Allen is different from many real politicians in that he is not well-known and therefore does not have some of the political baggage other politicians have, his partisanship is laid out clearly for all respondents, which should make him considerably polarizing for partisan individuals. Yet this is not what the results show. By making a credible empathetic appeal—tying his story to the story of those in his family who have struggled before him—even individuals from the opposing party begin to have positive attitudes toward his candidacy.

In addition to this, Allen is not hurt by making an empathetic appeal. He never performs significantly worse making an empathetic appeal rather than a sympathetic one, and his evaluations improve among co-partisans as well as those in the opposing party when empathy is evoked. Running on messages of empathy, then, is good politics, creating at least a modest incentive for reaching across the partisan divide.

3.6 Emotional Empathy

While experience is perhaps the most obvious way voters perceive empathy, another type of empathy is often the one we see discussed in the day-to-day events of a campaign. Emotional empathy refers to the idea that a candidate feels the same way Americans feel about the problems facing the country and its people. If Americans are generally comfortable with how things are in government, then successful politicians should evoke contentment and campaign on platforms that are concerned with maintaining American prosperity. Yet this is not how we generally view government. Negativity bias often creates an electoral atmosphere where maintaining the status quo is an unappealing message (Weaver 1986). Moreover, the partisan gridlock in Washington that marks the polarized era has made it incumbent upon most politicians for office to express some level of dissatisfaction with the status quo. It is in this expression of dissatisfaction that emotional empathy helps politicians connect with voters and convey the importance of both their participation and their voting decisions in the election. In the 2016 presidential primaries, Donald Trump and Bernie Sanders shared little in common politically, yet they were both insurgent candidates riding a wave of discontentment. In their respective primaries, there was relatively little to differentiate them policy-wise from their numerous opponents. The common perception was that each was appealing to a bloc of voters who felt dissatisfied and angry with status quo politics in Washington.

Yet candidates are not only noteworthy for times when they connect emotionally with an audience but also for times they fall flat. When political pundits refer to a candidate as "out of touch," they are often referencing the politician's personal style and emotional means of connecting with his or her audience. It is frequently interpreted as an indication that the candidate for office is not sufficiently motivated to bring about the change the American people want. As Mark Halperin and John Heilemann (2013) described Mitt Romney's 2012 bid for the presidency, much of the time and energy of those working on the campaign went into combatting the idea that Romney was an "unfeeling, out-of-touch fat cat" (410). Numerous anecdotes circulated about Romney throughout the campaign. Democratic and Republican opponents alike attacked his record at Bain Capital for making him appear unfeeling toward the working class, yet the critical narrative extended from Romney the businessman to Romney the person. For example, journalists and political opponents seized on a story that had circulated for years about an infamous Romney family road trip in which they ran out of space in the car and decided to tie the family dog Seamus's cage to the roof of the car.[23] Perhaps even more damning than the story itself was the lack of emotion Romney displayed when discussing these stories. When asked by the *Wall Street Journal* to explain his reasoning behind tying the dog to the roof of the car, Romney's response was simply, "Oh please, I've had a lot of dogs, and I care for them very deeply."[24] When Seamus made a mess during his roof-of-the-car trip (which may be the politest way to put it), Romney's hometown paper, the *Boston Globe*, reported that he hosed down the dog and the car to clean things off. As the *Globe* summarized, "It was a tiny preview of a trait he would

---

[23] "Mitt Romney's dog-on-the-car-roof story still proves to be his critics' best friend," *Washington Post*, March 14, 2012.

[24] Mitt Romney interview by *Wall Street Journal* editorial board, June 21, 2011.

grow famous for in business: emotion-free crisis management."[25] The story, and Romney's tepid defense of these actions, did little to quiet his critics.[26]

In 2016, many believed that Donald Trump would be done in by his lack of empathy for everyday Americans. Trump, born to a wealthy real estate developer and owner of the Miss Universe Pageant, had few experiences that would resonate with most Americans. Yet the emotionally empathetic cue made Trump an attractive politician to many. His brash demeanor and tell-it-like-it-is attitude won over a large majority of America's white working-class voters who were angry with the status quo, while Hillary Clinton's years in Washington and ties to the banking industry did not provide a strong contrast with Trump's wealthy background. Though neither Clinton nor Trump found themselves greatly advantaged in terms of experiential empathy, Trump was consistently perceived as more authentic because of the emotional aspect of his candidacy. Whereas Mitt Romney failed to connect on an emotional level with would-be supporters, many of whom were angry with the Obama administration, Trump connected because he appeared to feel the same anger his supporters felt.

The emotional aspect of empathy conveys a sense of urgency about the current moment. In 2012, why would a voter, especially one who is normally disinterested in politics, feel motivated to throw Barack Obama out of office if the man running against him didn't appear emotionally invested in the fight? The same could be asked of John Kerry, who similarly had to fight the perception that he was out of touch, not only because of his personal wealth but also because of his perceived lack of emotion. Voters are turned off by this kind of robotic demeanor because it implies the politician is, in some way, not particularly motivated to change the status quo. If empathy is an attractive trait in a politician, as I posit, because it implies that the politician will not only be qualified to solve a problem but also *motivated* to solve the problems facing average Americans, then emotional empathy is critical in addressing motivation.

Anger is a useful illustration of emotional empathy, but it is not the only one nor is it available equally to all politicians (see, e.g., Banks 2014; Phoenix 2019). Barack Obama's message of hope and Bill Clinton's pain felt for less fortunate individuals are strong examples of emotional empathy as well.

---

[25] "Journeys of a shared life," *Boston Globe*, June 27, 2007.
[26] Brian Fung, "The uncanny valley: What robot theory tells us about Mitt Romney," *The Atlantic*, January 31, 2012.

The example of Bill Clinton further shows how the dimensions of empathy can reinforce one another. Clinton had experiences that lent credibility to his claims of caring, yet he also exuded a pain in recalling those experiences that reinforced his connection with voters. Because candidates communicate empathy through commonality, it is essential that the voters perceive in a candidate the same emotion they already feel themselves. This leads to an additional hypothesis:

> H3. Emotional Empathy→ Compassion Hypothesis: When an individual feels
> a particular emotion with regard to politics, they will perceive a politician
> who shares that emotion as relatively more compassionate than one who does
> not share that emotion.

Study 2—Emotional Empathy

The second experiment I examine looks at the effect of emotional resonance, or a shared emotional orientation toward government between politician and respondent, on perceptions of compassion. I hypothesize that citizens perceive empathy in a politician when they feel the way the politician appears to feel. I administered the survey August 1–2, 2019, on a sample of 1,000 respondents via Amazon's Mechanical Turk (MTurk).[27] The survey first asked respondents how they felt about the American government and politics in general. Respondents could rate how angry, anxious, enthusiastic, or hopeful they felt from "not at all" to "a great deal" (a 1–4 scale). In order to have a measure for how relatively angry or hopeful each person was, I classified individuals as being "more angry" if they said they felt more angry than hopeful toward government, "more hopeful" if the opposite was true, or "neutral" if they said they felt equally angry and hopeful about politics. Respondents were then randomly assigned to receive a message from David Allen designed to be similar to the previous experiment. One message evoked hope and the other message evoked anger, but they were otherwise identical:

---

[27] Despite the non-random nature of the sampling procedure, the literature on experimental research using MTurk finds that researchers can make credible inferences regarding the relationships between treatments and outcomes of interest (Berinsky, Huber, and Lenz 2012).

Anger/Hope Treatment: David Allen, a local grocery store owner, is running for a seat in the U.S. House of Representatives as a [DEMOCRAT/ REPUBLICAN]. In his first public speech since filing to run for office, Allen spoke of his [ANGER AND IRRITATION/HOPE AND OPTIMISM] about the state of the nation as his reason for running. Allen told the crowd, "When I see what's happening in this country, I can't help but feel [TICKED OFF/ HOPEFUL]. I believe the time has come for people to step up and do something. I'm running for Congress because I know I can get something done for everyday Americans. I am asking each and every one of you for your vote this upcoming November election."

The difference between the anger and hope treatments had to be somewhat subtle to maintain the internal validity of the experiment. Often, candidates who appear angry identify the precise features of government that serve as the source of their anger (such as unfair trade policies or the premature and avoidable deaths of those who lack health insurance). Candidates who appear hopeful, on the other hand, often hold up the strength of the American people as their source for hope and ignore Washington politics, since Washington politics are more often a source of anger and frustration. Bringing these ideas into the vignettes would likely have made the treatments stronger and more realistic, but they would no longer have been different purely on the basis of the emotion evoked. As a result, I focus the manipulations in this experiment on mentions of the emotion and make sure the remaining text is identical.

Results

I test the emotional empathy → compassion hypothesis by looking specifically at shared characteristics between citizen and candidate. Here, I examine the impact of emotional resonance, which I define as instances in which the voter and the politician feel the same way about government and politics in general. Again, I argue that those who share the emotion of a politician will be more likely to perceive that politician as empathetic.

Before turning to the impact of emotional empathy on perceptions of compassion, I first consider the role that partisanship plays in the emotional orientation Americans feel toward government. Whether the party of an individual is in power or out of power should play a major role in how they feel about government at any given point in time. Furthermore, any politician who wishes to tap into a strong emotion in the American electorate must first be able to read the emotion of the American electorate, or

Table 3.1 Emotions of Partisans Toward Politics in 2019 MTurk Survey

	More Angry	Neutral	More Hopeful
Democrats (*N*=527)	70.6%	15.9%	13.5%
Republican (*N*=342)	42.8%	22.1%	35.1%
Independent (*N*=119)	61.8%	21.8%	16.4%

at least of their electoral constituency. After eight years of President Obama, Donald Trump was effectively able to tap into an anger and frustration felt widely in the Republican Party. Compared to Jeb Bush, whose more reserved demeanor earned him the nickname "low-energy Jeb,"[28] Trump appeared angrier and more motivated to take on the political establishment. At the time, Republicans appeared to respond positively to Trump's outbursts of anger. At the time of this survey's administration, however, emotions had shifted.

Table 3.1 shows how Democrats, Republicans, and independents[29] rated their feelings toward government and politics in general. There is a clear negativity bias, with pluralities across all partisan groups feeling more angry than hopeful. But among Democrats, an overwhelming majority of more than 70% said they felt greater anger than hope toward government, while less than 43% of Republicans said the same.

Turning now to whether a shared emotion drives positive perceptions of compassion and favorability, I examine ratings of David Allen on the "cares about people like you" item based on whether emotional resonance is present. Figure 3.3 shows that emotional resonance, defined as sharing the emotion the candidate is evoking, leads to more positive evaluations of compassion than when the politician evokes an opposing emotion.

Among all respondents, emotional resonance appears to increase perceptions that a candidate is truly compassionate. Among respondents who were more angry than hopeful about government, the anger candidate received higher evaluations on compassion by a margin of 4 percentage points. Among those who were more hopeful, the hope candidate was

[28] Matt Yglesias, "'Low-Energy': Donald Trump's favorite diss on Jeb Bush, explained," *Vox*, September 4, 2015.
[29] "Independent leaners," or those who claim to be politically independent but admit to leaning toward the Democratic or Republican Party, are grouped with partisans.

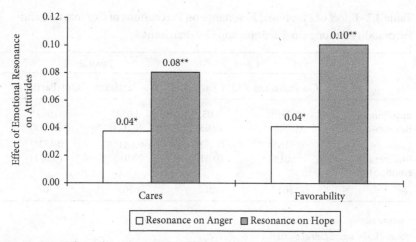

Figure 3.3 Effect of Emotional Resonance on Perceptions of Compassion by Partisanship
*Effects are statistically significant at $p<0.05$
**Effects are statistically significant at $p<0.01$

perceived as more compassionate by an even greater margin of 8 percentage points.

The results on favorability show that a shared emotional orientation toward government not only influences perceptions of compassion but overall candidate favorability as well. These results largely mirror those on perceptions of compassion, with resonance on hope showing a somewhat stronger effect, but with resonance on both emotions providing a significant boost to public opinion. And although treatment effects are not overwhelming, it is important to keep in mind that these treatments were, by necessity, subtle. Whereas Donald Trump's anger in 2016 was almost always directed at establishment politicians and Barack Obama's optimism in 2008 was almost always directed at the American people, these treatments did not identify a source for the emotion.

Does the sincerity barrier also play a role when it comes to messages conveying emotion rather than experience? To assess this, I again operationalize this barrier using partisanship, since partisans should be most skeptical of the claims made by out-partisans. I consider whether out-partisans respond more strongly than co-partisans to emotional resonance (Table 3.2). Unlike messages regarding experience, the effect of emotional resonance is roughly the same (and not statistically distinguishable) regardless of whether the politician is a co-partisan. This is

Table 3.2 Effect of Emotional Resonance on Perceptions of Compassion and Favorability Among Co-Partisans and Out-Partisans

	Cares		Favorability	
	Co-Partisans	Out-Partisans	Co-Partisans	Out-Partisans
Emotional Resonance	0.055* (0.020)	0.051* (0.031)	0.053* (0.023)	0.062* (0.029)
Constant (different emotion)	0.615** (0.014)	0.453** (0.013)	0.641** (0.016)	0.453** (0.021)
N	363	367	363	367

*Statistically significant at $p<.05$
**Statistically significant at $p<.01$

likely because respondents are no longer evaluating a sympathetic candidate relative to an empathetic candidate where particular claims of caring are deemed credible or not. Instead, all forms of emotional resonance fit the description of empathy rather than sympathy due to a commonality to bond the politician and the survey respondent. As a result emotional resonance has a roughly equal effect regardless of the partisanship of the politician and the respondent. Importantly, emotional resonance helps politicians connect with citizens regardless of whether they share the same party, meaning emotional empathy is not exclusively a tool for energizing one's electoral base.

3.7 Identity-Based Empathy

Sharing similar experiences and emotions are critical ways in which common bonds are formed between politicians and those they represent. With identity, a third pathway, shared experiences and emotions can be conveyed without an explicit appeal. When the voters and the candidate share salient identities, it can communicate the candidate's ability to understand how individuals live and the belief systems that dominate their thought processes.

The common way scholars measure empathy is through the survey item that gauges whether a politician "cares about people like you." While I have argued that "cares" is a term loaded with meaning and can be divided along dimensions of sympathy and empathy, the phrase "like you" is equally important in determining how an individual will respond to the question.

Who precisely belongs in the group of "people like you" can vary from person to person, but we know that particular characteristics, such as race, religion, and sexual orientation, are especially salient in influencing political attitudes (Green, Palmquist, and Schickler 2002; Frable 1997; Huddy 2001; Miller et al. 1981; Tate 2003). In this way, empathy is not only about a personal connection; it is also about a connection to a group. Voters do not get to know politicians on a personal level, but instead must estimate their likelihood of delivering on their promises for "people like me" through their attributes and the messages they transmit. This also highlights the self-interested nature of empathy when it comes to American politics. Experiential and emotional empathy may be thought of in normatively desirable ways: as a connection that shows a politician is genuine in his or her promises to people who are struggling or who feel a particular way about how government functions. Yet empathy is also about how the government distributes resources. These resources are finite, and voters want to know that they and others who they perceive as the most deserving will be taken care of. When a politician is a member of the in-group for a salient identity, whether it is race, gender, religion, etc., it signals to voters that they will take care of those people who are also part of that group. Thus, identity-based empathy is closely related to theories of in-group bias and out-group prejudice.

Shared salient identities are perhaps more important in the modern political era than ever before. In the mid-20th century, cross-cutting identities mitigated the power of partisanship. White southern Protestants found themselves tenuously aligned with northern Catholics and Jews vying for control of the Democratic Party. With the civil rights movement, however, white Protestants became increasingly associated with the Republican Party, effectively sorting the parties into more clearly defined groups without cross-cutting identities. This socio-partisan sorting has left both parties more homogenous, eliminating the cross-pressures that used to moderate an individual's partisanship. While identity politics has historically been used to describe the Democratic Party's coalition (Mason and Wronski 2018), this is no longer true in the modern era. The Democratic coalition, which had largely been characterized as a collection of historically marginalized groups (i.e. African Americans, Catholics, women, etc.), is now no more driven by identity than the Republican coalition (see Jardina 2019 for a discussion of white identity politics). As white Protestants shifted dramatically to the

Republican Party, both party labels took on the characteristics of a strong social identity, both in terms of in-group preference and out-group resentment
(e.g., Iyengar and Krupenkin 2018; Mason and Wronski 2018).

With the strengthening of partisan affect, voters themselves have evolved
in what they want and expect from leaders who represent them. Voters
largely support candidates who represent them descriptively and provide
for their subjective interests (Barreto, Segura, and Woods 2004; Rouse 2013;
Tate 2003). Although the desire for descriptive representation goes well beyond empathy, empathy remains a key component. Many Black voters believe that their ultimate well-being is enhanced when the entire group is
better off (Dawson 1994), and no white politician could possibly empathize
with the Black experience in America to the same degree as a Black politician. With the rise of affective polarization, white group identity similarly
fuels the degree to which white rural voters believe a politician can truly empathize with them. As Cramer (2016) points out, white rural voters see government as favoring those in urban communities, which are far more racially
diverse and reflective of the Democratic Party coalition. White politicians,
then, will be seen by this group as better able to correct for this imbalance,
understanding and caring about the needs of white voters in a way a non-
white politician could not. Moreover, with the rise of negative partisanship,
or the tendency of many to develop a partisan identity largely in opposition
to the party or parties they dislike (Iyengar and Krupenkin 2018), it is no
surprise that white Republicans might be turned off by a party that is seen
as representing a different set of interests. As the Republican Party becomes
associated with white Protestantism, Republicans should be more supportive
of those candidates who look and act like those in the Protestant community.

For Mike Huckabee, part of his appeal was experiential, but a significant
portion of his appeal was based on his membership in groups critical to the
Republican Party. Yes, he grew up poor and understood what it was like to
struggle. When he advocated for a smaller government, voters might be
more readily convinced that he was not approaching it from the perspective that he simply wanted to provide corporations and those at the very top
the ability to keep more of their money. Instead, they could view his policy
position through the prism of experience—Huckabee felt that this approach
was the best way to help those in his community who were not wealthy and
did not possess great political influence. Yet identity lent further credibility
to Huckabee's claims. His strong credentials as a southern Baptist pastor
and an evangelical Christian were an added cue to socially conservative

Republicans that he was sincere in his desire to bring Christian values to the White House. In this way, Mike Huckabee would have been able to win over some voters without emphasizing his humble beginnings, because he would already be trusted by those who shared his evangelical Christian identity, an identity salient for many in the Republican Party in determining voter choice (Layman 1997).

With race, the empathetic cue is even more straightforward. All experiences we have as individuals are strongly tied to our racial identities, such that those who are co-ethnic or co-racial have undoubtedly had experiences similar to our own. In part, this explains why congressional districts overwhelmingly choose politicians who belong to the same racial group as the majority of their voters (Mansbridge 1999; Pitkin 1967; Swain 1993). While many factors play into this, race provides a cue to voters about what issues and what types of people will be first and foremost in the minds of the politicians when they craft policy. Dawson's theory of linked fate (1994) suggests that race can be more important than personal experience in determining one's vote, as even wealthy Black voters will support the candidate they believe will be better for the group as a whole. And although a host of different identities can generate a sense of linked fate and group consciousness (Gay, Hochschild, and White 2016), race and ethnicity are salient identities not only for those belonging to historically marginalized racial groups (Sanchez and Vargas 2016; Simien 2005; Stout, Kretschmer, and Ruppanner , 2017; Tate 1993) but for white Americans as well (Jardina 2019). These identities lead to anger when the group is mistreated and motivate political action on behalf of the group as a whole.

Perhaps no example in modern history better illustrates the power of race than Barack Obama. Obama's personal history did not lend itself well to the narrative that he had a particularly strong understanding of the average Black experience in America. As Ta-Nehisi Coates put it, "Obama is biracial, and has a direct connection with Africa. He is articulate, young, and handsome. He does not feel the need to yell, 'Reparations now!' into any available microphone."[30]

Coates and others in the Black community were referencing the uniqueness of Obama. Obama spent time in his childhood in Indonesia, was raised by white grandparents in Hawaii, and attended private schools. He graduated

[30] Ta-Nehisi Coates, "Is Obama Black enough?," *Time*, February 1, 2007.

from Columbia University and Harvard Law School. His struggles were not viewed by many as emblematic of the Black experience in America. Yet for all this, Barack Obama was something that no other major party presidential nominee had ever been: non-white. Black voters, then, could see in a presidential candidate an identity that held special importance to them. For Obama and Black voters, race could serve as a cue that he understood the unique burden imposed on the Black minority in the United States. This cue was undoubtedly important in influencing support for Obama, but it has also translated into support for a number of other candidates for public office.

While it is not often put in these terms, identity politics has a close relationship with candidate empathy. With regard to this, I argue that genuine empathy is one of the most important reasons that voters want descriptive representation in government. Americans want individuals in the highest offices who do not need a crash course in the problems most Americans face. They want someone who is both aware of the problems and sufficiently motivated to solve them. Experience with a problem provides a politician with awareness. Emotion indicates to voters a desire to do something to solve the problem. With identity, there is both; a voter can infer that they have had experiences similar to a politician, and they can infer that the politician will be motivated to help those people who belong to that group as well. In that way, group interest serves as a proxy for self-interest. As a result, I offer the following hypothesis:

> H4. Identity-Based Empathy → Compassion Hypothesis: An individual who shares a politically salient identity with a politician will perceive that politician as more compassionate than a politician who does not share that identity.

Study 3—Identity-Based Empathy

I examine the impact of sharing a salient identity on perceptions of compassion by using an experiment nearly identical to the previous two. I administered the survey July 14–16, 2018, on a sample of 665 MTurk respondents. As in the previous experiments, respondents for this survey also read a story about congressional candidate David Allen making a plea for votes. The text to the vignette was identical to the control condition for Experiment 1. Yet for this experiment, I attached a picture to the treatment that varied the race of David Allen as either white or Black. Because some will infer partisanship based on the race of the politician (Karl and Ryan 2016; Jones 2014), the survey vignette explicitly stated that David Allen was a Democrat. The sample was limited to only white and Black respondents, with an oversample of Black respondents in order to examine how white and Black respondents react to co-racial candidates.[31] To ensure that white and Black respondents received a roughly similar number of co-racial versus different race appeals, I block randomized assignment to the two treatments by the race of the respondent.[32] For every respondent, I constructed a variable based on whether the appeal they received was "co-racial," or coming from a politician who shared the same race as the respondent.

The identity-based empathy → compassion hypothesis states that individuals will perceive a politician as more compassionate if they share a salient political identity. Unlike experiences and emotions, many of the most salient identities are highly visible. And while many identities are politically relevant and are likely to determine the degree to which an individual views a politician as empathetic, I choose to focus on race as a source of identity-based empathy. I do this both for simplicity's sake and because race is one of the most historically important political identities (e.g., Dawson 1994; Tate 2003). I hypothesize that individuals who belong to the same racial group as David Allen will view him as more compassionate. Yet I also recognize that race may not be salient for everyone, so I also examine the findings by partisanship. Prior research shows that one of the important drivers of identity importance is social sorting (Mason 2015), so racial identities should be stronger among those whose race and party align (e.g., white Republicans, Black Democrats). Respondents who do not belong to the same racial group as David Allen or who do not view their race as an important identity should view him as relatively less compassionate, even when partisanship is being held constant.

Results
I first examine the effect of a co-racial candidate on perceived compassion across white and Black respondents. Sharing the same race as the politician

---

[31] The sampling procedure yielded 300 Black respondents and 365 white respondents.

[32] Among the 300 Black respondents in the sample, 148 received the white candidate treatment, while 152 received the Black candidate treatment. Among the 365 white respondents in the sample, 184 received the Black candidate treatment and 181 received the white candidate treatment.

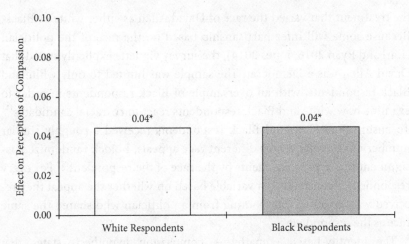

Figure 3.4 Effect of Co-Racial Politician on Perceptions of Compassion
*Effects are statistically significant at $p<0.05$

leads to significantly more positive evaluations on compassion (Figure 3.4). Overall, co-racial candidates receive about 4 percentage points more positive evaluations on the trait of compassion. For the total sample it is clear that the race of the candidate on its own is enough to cue voters whether a politician is truly compassionate toward people like them.

Although this finding provides support for the identity-based empathy hypothesis, the substantive effects are relatively small. Figures 3.5, however, helps explain the muted effects. Among Republicans, whiteness appears to play a critical role in how the candidates are evaluated. When David Allen is presented as a Black Democrat, white Republicans rate him an average of 0.47 (from 0 to 1) on compassion. Although Allen was described as uncontroversial, this rating is reasonably high given that Allen is described as a Black Democrat. Yet when Allen is presented as white instead of Black, that rating skyrockets by roughly 15 percentage points. Even in an era of high polarization, where Democrats and Republicans are at the very least thought to view each other with suspicion if not downright animosity, white Republicans view the white Democrat as, on average, generally caring about people like them. Republicans are far more willing to give Allen the benefit of the doubt that he cares about people like them when he is a white Democrat rather than a Black Democrat. Race, when aligned with partisanship, clearly plays a strong role in determining whether a politician is viewed as compassionate.[33]

---

[33] There were an insufficient number of Black Republicans in the sample for analyses of that group.

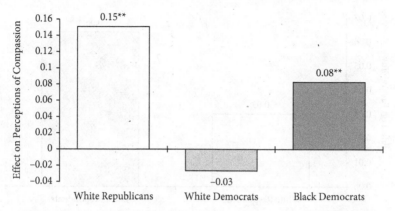

Figure 3.5 Effect of Co-Racial Politician on Perceptions of Compassion by Partisanship
**Effects are statistically significant at $p<0.01$

For white Democrats, the white politician fares no better than the Black politician. This is precisely the same finding as those found in the previous chapter, where white Democrats did not differentiate between Chris Van Hollen and Donna Edwards. Because the Democratic Party coalition is more racially diverse and less reliant on the white vote, white Democrats are in many ways out of alignment. The white vote has increasingly shifted toward the Republican Party, putting white Democrats' racial and partisan identities at odds. When politically important social identities are out of alignment, Mason (2018) argues, it results in cross-pressured groups that will be less likely to use race as an important filter for assessing politicians and political events. For respondents low in white identity (Jardina 2019), expectations are weaker as to how whiteness should inform their evaluations of candidates. White Democrats examined here, then, likely feel a weaker attachment to their race than white Republicans, whose party relies far more on the white voting bloc and has come to be associated with representing the interests of white Americans. Black Democrats evaluating a Black Democratic politician, however, rate the politician much more positively on compassion than they do the white Democratic politician.

Figures 3.6 and 3.7 show similar analyses on measures of general favorability. Shared racial identity, not surprisingly, leads generally to greater levels of support for both white and Black respondents (Figure 3.6). Looking at this by party affiliation, we see support for the assertion that when partisanship aligns with other salient identities, it plays an important role in how the voters perceive the politician (Figure 3.7). White Democrats give David

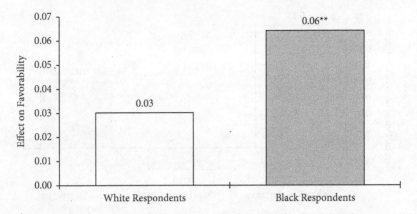

Figure 3.6 Effect of Co-Racial Politician on Favorability
**Effects are statistically significant at $p<0.01$

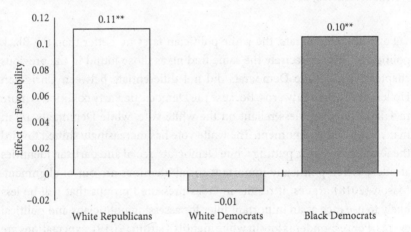

Figure 3.7 Effect of Co-Racial Politician on Favorability by Partisanship
**Effects are statistically significant at $p<0.01$

Allen nearly identical ratings regardless of his race. For Black respondents, however, the gap is substantively massive at 10 percentage points. These results indicate that Black Democrats should have a built-in advantage when it comes to primary voting. White Democrats do not appear to penalize a Black politician for not sharing the same race, while Black Democrats advantage the Black politician.

Yet this advantage evaporates in a general election when Republicans are evaluating the candidate. White Republicans react in an opposite direction from white Democrats. Overall, white Republicans are very mixed with regard to David Allen when he is presented as a white Democrat, with an average rating of 0.48 (0–1 scale). This is 11 percentage points better than when Allen is presented as a Black Democrat. These findings point to a major hurdle for multiracial democracy in the United States—it is hard for politicians to reach across the partisan divide if it coincides with the racial divide.

That race is an important determinant of political behavior and electoral fortunes is not a novel finding of this research (see, e.g., Piston 2010). What is novel, however, is the insight that an important ingredient in the role that race plays in American public opinion comes down to perceptions of compassion. A Black politician does not need to make any kind of explicit appeal to Black voters to be perceived as caring more about Black people (at least relative to a white candidate). In a Democratic primary, this phenomenon may be critical. A Black candidate does not pay a cost in perceptions of compassion or favorability among white Democrats but does receive a benefit among the important Black Democratic constituency. Conversely, a white Democrat can more effectively appeal to white Republicans in a general election than a Black Democrat can. Although not tested directly here, this phenomenon is likely to persist across multiple identities that are associated with the two parties (such as those based on religion, sexual orientation, or class). This has important implications for the types of candidates we see win primaries and the costs they might face in the general election.

3.8 Race and the 2008 Election of Barack Obama

Examining the various dimensions of empathy using experimental data provides a number of important advantages for causal inferences. Yet, as I discussed in Chapter 2, observational data provide the greatest advantage for showing that the experimental findings extend to real-world situations.

In 2008, the nomination of Barack Obama meant that, for the first time, one of the two major presidential contenders was Black. This change provided a glimpse into the role racial identity can play in determining whether a voter believes a candidate cares about people like them. If partisanship, ideology, or policy, and not salient identities like race determined the degree to which an individual perceives compassion in a candidate, we should expect that Democrats of all races would see Obama as similar in his capacity for compassion as other Democratic candidates that came before.

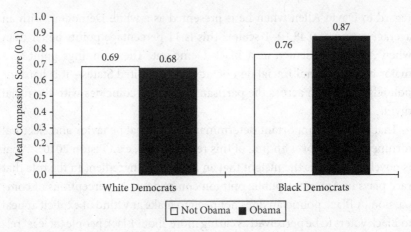

Figure 3.8 Perceptions of Democratic Candidate Compassion by Race
Source: American National Election Studies, 1992–2020 (values are weighted)

Figure 3.8 shows this not to be the case. Here I show how white and Black Democrats rated the various Democratic presidential nominees in terms of compassion, normalizing their ratings on a 0–1 scale. Among white Democrats, Obama is perceived as equally compassionate with other Democratic candidates from 1992 to 2020. For white Democrats, who are out of alignment when it comes to race and partisanship, it appears that partisanship wins out just as it did in the case of the Maryland Senate primary and in the identity-based empathy experiment. Regardless of the source of the data, it appears that white Democrats do not view race as a key commonality when differentiating between Democratic politicians.

Black Democrats, however, *do* use race to differentiate between the candidates. The difference among Black Democrats is more than 10 points. Considering the already high rating Black Democrats give to all Democratic presidential candidates, this positive shift for Obama is especially noteworthy, suggesting race and empathy are closely related. Though Black Democrats generally view the Democratic nominee as compassionate, Obama was exceptional in this regard. Having a co-racial candidate for office, then, appears to play an important role in determining why certain politicians excel in evaluations of empathy.

3.9 Summary

In this chapter, I have sought to lay out and test a theory of political compassion. The empirical analyses show that Americans base their evaluations of candidate compassion on the quantity and intensity of commonalities that link them to the politician in question. Although the potential sources of commonality are numerous, I have provided a simple classification scheme for the commonalities voters often deem relevant, which includes common experiences, emotions, and identities. All of these common traits are pow-erful determinants of perceptions of compassion.

From the perspectives of voters, these results are straightforward. They seek out and support candidates they believe better understand their problems and care about them. They want a leader who is not only aware of the concerns and anxieties they face in their day-to-day lives but who can also feel those concerns and anxieties as if those emotions were their own. This is made easier when the politician has had the same experiences as the voter, exudes the same emotion as the voter, or holds the same identities as the voter.

The implications from the perspective of politicians and campaigns are somewhat less clear. Certainly, a candidate will be best served if she can dem-onstrate a clear linkage between herself and the voters through experience, emotion, and identity, yet these practices come with risk. I have shown that credible empathetic appeals serve to increase perceptions of compassion among voters, yet not every candidate can make a credible empathetic appeal in all circumstances. Mitt Romney, for example, struggled to find experiences in his background that resonated with working- or middle-class Americans. Hillary Clinton often pointed to her mother's experiences as a child as a pri-mary motivation for her political life,[34] yet the speeches she gave to Goldman Sachs and other Wall Street firms made it seem like she might be more in-terested in enriching herself than helping others (something I examine in greater detail in Chapter 5).[35] My research shows, however, that even when a credible empathetic appeal is not possible, making a sympathetic appeal can still generate a positive public image, especially among co-partisans. For politicians like Romney and Clinton, being viewed as truly empathetic may be difficult but being viewed as sympathetic may buttress some of the nega-tivity on perceptions of compassion.

The findings here suggest emotional appeals have the greatest impact on perceptions of compassion, but they must be employed with similar skill to be successful. Donald Trump was able to tap into much of the anger in the Republican base, yet few observers would suspect that his anger was

---

[34] Hillary Clinton Campaign ad, "Family Strong," August 2, 2015.
[35] "Sanders rips Clinton over Goldman Sachs ties," *The Hill*, January 17, 2016.

inauthentic. If a politician is not truly angry or hopeful, it may be difficult for them to feign that emotion believably. Personal style, then, is a critical feature for this pathway to empathy. Donald Trump had been known for his bluster long before running for public office. Someone like John Kerry, by contrast, was viewed by the public more as a statesman. He had a lengthy political career prior to his presidential candidacy, an Ivy League education, and, as the *Los Angeles Times* put it, "a patrician pedigree."[36] While there was a portion of the electorate in 2004 that was likely angry with George W. Bush's presidency, Kerry's style was ill-suited to tap into that anger.

Similarly, politicians must be able to accurately read the emotions of the American electorate. As the survey evidence showed, emotions are closely related to the partisanship of the individual and the party that is in power. Democrats in 2019 were overwhelmingly angry, while Republicans were on average far more hopeful. Democratic candidates at that time who exuded anger likely had a major advantage over primary opponents that struck a hopeful tone. The independents in the sample, though small in number, also reflected an anger with status quo politics in the United States, suggesting that angry candidates in a general election are likely to have a leg-up on the competition. But the emotional sentiment of the electorate changes over time, and politicians must be able to shift course when the broader political environment becomes more optimistic or pessimistic.

Finally, I showed that politicians who share salient identities with voters are perceived as more compassionate. The analyses also suggest that the effect of a shared identity is stronger when that identity is aligned with partisanship. White Republicans and Black Democrats strongly differentiate between candidates based on race, while white Democrats do not.

These three experiments suggest that commonalities both drive up perceptions of compassion *and* translate into more favorable general impressions. When coupled with the findings in the previous chapter, which leveraged observational data examining real-world elections, the cumulative evidence points to the importance of campaign-messaging strategies. There has been a great deal of debate over whether campaigns matter, especially in a polarized era where fewer persuadable voters are out there. The last two chapters show that perceptions of compassion can play an important,

---

[36] "Politics with an Irish accent," *Los Angeles Times*, July 30, 2004.

often decisive, role in voting decisions and election outcomes, and these perceptions are malleable, prone to persuasion and manipulation by the campaigns themselves. Yet the experiments described thus far have sought to eliminate any complicating or intervening factors beyond experience, emotion, and racial identity. In the real world, however, messages related to compassion often have a gendered meaning, such that empathetic messages may be received differently if they come from a man or a woman. Although gender is often not as salient an identity as race among most citizens, research shows that voters subscribe to gender stereotypes that may constrain the effect of campaign messages from women running for office. I turn to a study of these dynamics in the next chapter.

Appendix: Survey Design, Instruments, and Results

Empirical Approach

In all three surveys, respondents read about David Allen, a fictional congressional candidate running for office in the upcoming election. In an attempt to maintain a high level of ecological validity, respondents were told that David Allen was running for Congress outside of the respondent's district.

In the three experiments, respondents rated David Allen on the same evaluations (full wording can be found below in this appendix). Following the vignettes, respondents were asked to rate the degree to which they agreed with the statement that David Allen "really cares about people like you." Respondents also rated the degree to which they had a favorable or unfavorable view of Allen. For ease of interpretation, both of these dependent variables in the following analyses have been normalized from 0 to 1 so that differences between groups can be interpreted as the percentage point change across the response scale.

By randomly assigning respondents to the treatment and control conditions, I examine support for David Allen across messages simply by comparing mean levels of support for the candidate across all conditions in all three experiments. The random assignment of subjects to the treatments across all the experiments was successful. Due to the success of random assignment to the conditions, differences in the dependent variable across conditions can be attributed to the manipulation rather than potential confounders (Kinder and Palfrey 1993).

2016 SSI Experiment: Experiential Empathy

Treatment Wording

Control: David Allen, a local grocery store owner, is running for a seat in the U.S. House of Representatives as a Democrat (Republican). He is forty-eight years old and has two children with his wife of twenty years. While he has long been a prominent citizen in his community and active in local politics, this is the first time he has run for Congress. In his first public speech since filing to run for office, Allen told the crowd, "I am asking each and every one of you for your vote this upcoming November election."

Sympathy: David Allen, a local grocery store owner, is running for a seat in the U.S. House of Representatives as a Democrat (Republican). He is forty-eight years old and has two children with his wife of twenty years. While he has long been a prominent citizen in his community and active in local politics, this is the first time he has run for Congress. In his first public speech since filing to run for office, Allen spoke of how much he cares about struggling families as his motivation for running. Allen told the crowd, "I care about the neighborhood mailmen and the part-time secretaries. I've heard the stories of grandfathers who worked as coal-miners to scratch out a living but couldn't even afford indoor plumbing. I've talked to families who have lived this hardship, and I care about those struggling to make ends meet. I'm running for Congress to help those Americans. I am asking each and every one of you for your vote this upcoming November election."

Empathy: David Allen, a local grocery store owner, is running for a seat in the U.S. House of Representatives as a Democrat (Republican). He is forty-eight years old and has two children with his wife of twenty years. While he has long been a prominent citizen in his community and active in local politics, this is the first time he has run for Congress. In his first public speech since filing to run for office, Allen spoke of his own history growing up in a struggling family as his motivation for running. Allen told the crowd, "My dad was the neighborhood mailman and my mom worked as a part-time secretary. My grandfather worked as a coal-miner to scratch out a living but couldn't even afford indoor plumbing. My family has lived this hardship, so I understand the struggles of those trying to make ends meet. I'm running for Congress to help those Americans. I am asking each and every one of you for your vote this upcoming November election."

Post-Treatment Question Wording

Overall, how favorable or unfavorable is your impression of David Allen?

1 Strongly Unfavorable
2 Somewhat Unfavorable
3 Somewhat Favorable
4 Strongly Favorable

Respondents then randomly assigned to read one of the following questions:[37]

Question 1:

In your opinion, does the phrase, "he really cares about people like you" describe David Allen extremely well, very well, moderately well, slightly well, or not well at all?

1 Extremely well
2 Very well
3 Moderately well
4 Slightly well
5 Not well at all

---

[37] Scholars involved in carrying out this study preferred the answer options offered in Question 2 of the questions, though the options in Set 1 reflect those most often used in well-respected surveys (such as the ANES). The results between those who received Question 1 and Question 2 were not appreciably different. In the later surveys, I employ only Question 2.

Question 2:

In your opinion, does the phrase, "he really cares about people like you" describe David Allen very well, somewhat well, neither well nor poorly, somewhat poorly, or extremely poorly?

1 Very well
· 2 Somewhat well
3 Neither well nor poorly
4 Somewhat poorly
5 Extremely poorly

Results

Table A3.1 Treatment Effects of Compassionate Appeals on Dependent Variables of Interest (Control as Baseline)

Condition	Cares (Full Sample)	Cares (Co-partisans)	Cares (Opp. Partisans)	Fav. (Full Sample)	Fav. (Co-partisans)	Fav. (Opp. Partisans
Sympathy Treatment (N=445)	0.112** (0.024)	0.120** (0.036)	0.063 (0.038)	0.113** (0.020)	0.099** (0.024)	0.116** (0.035)
Empathy Treatment (N=427)	0.162** (0.021)	0.174** (0.031)	0.168** (0.033)	0.114** (0.018)	0.086** (0.024)	0.175** (0.028)
Constant (Control) (N=560)	0.467** (0.014)	0.530** (0.021)	0.423** (0.024)	0.591** (0.013)	0.677** (0.018)	0.500 (0.022)
Prob>F	0.000	0.000	0.000	0.000	0.000	0.000
N	1,352	557	574	1,355	559	575

**Statistically significant at $p<.01$ (one-tailed test)

Table A3.2 Randomization Check—Multinomial Logit Predicting Assignment to Condition (Control as Omitted Category, Standard Errors in Parentheses)

Independent Variable	Sympathy Cond.	Empathy Cond.
Age	0.004	0.007
	(0.005)	(0.006)
Gender (Male)	0.078	−0.236
	(0.163)	(0.166)
Race (White)	−0.146	0.297
	(0.190)	(0.198)
Education	−0.008	−0.088
	(0.063)	(0.061)
Income	−0.019	0.020
	(0.032)	(0.031)
Ideology	−0.020	−0.038
	(0.059)	(0.064)
Partisanship	0.039	0.036
	(0.046)	(0.047)
Constant	−0.195	−0.379
	(0.489)	(0.485)
Chi-Square	0.421	
N	1,278	

2019 Amazon Mechanical Turk Experiment: Emotional Empathy

Treatment Wording

Anger/hope treatment: David Allen, a local grocery store owner, is running for a seat in the U.S. House of Representatives as a [DEMOCRAT/ REPUBLICAN]. In his first public speech since filing to run for office, Allen spoke of his [ANGER AND IRRITATION/HOPE AND OPTIMISM] about the state of the nation as his reason for running. Allen told the crowd, "When I see what's happening in this country, I can't help but feel [TICKED OFF/ HOPEFUL]. I believe the time has come for people to step up and do something. I'm running for Congress because I know I can get something done for everyday Americans. I am asking each and every one of you for your vote this upcoming November election."

Pre-Treatment Question Wording

Please rate how you feel about American government today and politics in general.

A. Angry
B. Anxious
C. Enthusiastic
D. Hopeful

Choices:

1 Not at all
2 Very little
3 Somewhat
4 A great deal

Post-Treatment Question Wording

Overall, how favorable or unfavorable is your impression of David Allen?

1 Strongly Unfavorable
2 Somewhat Unfavorable
3 Neither Favorable nor Unfavorable
4 Somewhat Favorable
5 Strongly Favorable

In your opinion, does the phrase, "he really cares about people like you" describe David Allen very well, somewhat well, neither well nor poorly, somewhat poorly, or extremely poorly?

1 Very well
2 Somewhat well
3 Neither well nor poorly
4 Somewhat poorly
5 Extremely poorly

Results

Table A3.3 Treatment Effects of Compassionate Appeals on Dependent Variables (Hopeful Candidate as Baseline)

Condition	Cares about People Like You			Favorability		
	Angry Respondent	Neutral Respondent	Hopeful Respondent	Angry Respondent	Neutral Respondent	Hopeful Respondent
Angry Candidate Treatment	0.038* (0.023)	-0.017 (0.038)	-0.080** (0.033)	0.041* (0.022)	-0.014 (0.035)	-0.101** (0.033)
Constant (Hopeful Candidate Treatment)	0.494** (0.016)	0.617** (0.027)	0.716** (0.022)	0.512** (0.015)	0.614** (0.024)	0.723** (0.022)
N	613	184	203	613	184	203

*Statistically significant at $p<.05$ (one-tailed test)

**Statistically significant at $p<.01$ (one-tailed test)

Table A3.4A Treatment Effects of Compassionate Appeals on Dependent Variables (Hopeful Candidate as Baseline)—Among Democrats

Condition	Cares About People Like You			Favorability		
	Angry Respondent	Neutral Respondent	Hopeful Respondent	Angry Respondent	Neutral Respondent	Hopeful Respondent
Angry Candidate Treatment	0.010 (0.028)	−0.037 (0.056)	−0.125** (0.050)	0.034 (0.027)	0.003 (0.052)	−0.100* (0.052)
Constant (Hopeful Candidate Treatment)	0.501** (0.020)	0.642** (0.041)	0.730** (0.036)	0.507** (0.019)	0.597** (0.038)	0.716 (0.038)
N	417	94	80	417	94	80

*Statistically significant at p<.05 (one-tailed test)

**Statistically significant at p<.01 (one-tailed test)

Table A3.4B Treatment Effects of Compassionate Appeals on Dependent Variables (Hopeful Candidate as Baseline) — Among Republicans

Condition	Cares About People Like You			Favorability		
	Angry Respondent	Neutral Respondent	Hopeful Respondent	Angry Respondent	Neutral Respondent	Hopeful Respondent
Angry Candidate Treatment	0.117**	0.015	-0.034	0.037	-0.038	-0.090*
	(0.047)	(0.059)	(0.046)	(0.044)	(0.054)	(0.047)
Constant (Hopeful Candidate Treatment)	0.496**	0.610**	0.721**	0.568**	0.647**	0.734**
	(0.032)	(0.041)	(0.030)	(0.031)	(0.038)	(0.030)
N	128	66	105	128	66	105

*Statistically significant at $p<.05$ (one-tailed test)

**Statistically significant at $p<.01$ (one-tailed test)

Table A3.5 Randomization Check—Logit Predicting
Assignment to Anger Condition (Hopeful Condition
as Omitted Category, Standard Errors in Parentheses)

Independent Variable	Anger Condition
Age	0.008
	(0.005)
Gender (Male)	0.164
	(0.130)
Race (White)	0.215
	(0.153)
Income	−0.001
	(0.020)
Partisanship	−0.048
	(0.031)
Constant	−0.416
	(0.277)
Chi-Square	0.201
N	998

2018 Amazon Mechanical Turk Experiment: Identity-Based Empathy

Treatment Wording

Introduction: Now we would like to get your opinion about a candidate running for Congress outside of your state. Please read the following excerpt from a newspaper article describing the announcement of his candidacy and then tell us what you think about him.

Black Candidate Treatment

David Allen, a local grocery store owner, is running for a seat in the U.S. House of Representatives as a Democrat. He is forty-eight years old and has two children with his wife of twenty years. While he has long been a prominent citizen in his community and active in local politics, this is the first time he has run for Congress. In his first public speech since filing to run for office, Allen told the crowd, "I am asking each and every one of you for your vote this upcoming November election."

David Allen

White Candidate Treatment

David Allen, a local grocery store owner, is running for a seat in the U.S. House of Representatives as a Democrat. He is forty-eight years old and has two children with his wife of twenty years. While he has long been a prominent citizen in his community and active in local politics, this is the first time he has run for Congress. In his first public speech since filing to run for office, Allen told the crowd, "I am asking each and every one of you for your vote this upcoming November election."

David Allen

Post-Treatment Question Wording

Overall, how favorable or unfavorable is your impression of David Allen?

1 Strongly Unfavorable
2 Somewhat Unfavorable
3 Somewhat Favorable
4 Strongly Favorable

In your opinion, does the phrase, "he really cares about people like you" describe David Allen

1 Very poorly
2 Somewhat poorly
3 Neither poorly nor well
4 Somewhat well
5 Very well

Results

Table A3.6 Treatment Effects of Co-Racial Candidate on Perceptions of Candidate Compassion

Condition	Full Sample	White Democrats	Black Democrats	White Republicans
Co-Racial (N=333)	0.045** (0.018)	−0.027 (0.030)	0.083** (0.030)	0.151** (0.044)
Constant (Different Race) (N=332)	0.604** (0.013)	0.694** (0.021)	0.619** (0.022)	0.470 (0.031)
N	665	188	209	131

**Statistically significant at $p<.01$ (one-tailed test)

Table A3.7 Treatment Effects of Co-Racial Candidate on Candidate Favorability

Condition	Full Sample	White Democrats	Black Democrats	White Republicans
Co-Racial (N=333)	0.046* (0.020)	−0.013 (0.029)	0.105** (0.030)	0.111* (0.052)
Constant (Different Race) (N=332)	0.594** (0.014)	0.710** (0.021)	0.643** (0.022)	0.373 (0.052)
N	665	188	209	131

*Statistically significant at $p<.05$ (one-tailed test)
**Statistically significant at $p<.01$ (one-tailed test)

Table A3.8 Randomization Check—Logit Predicting Assignment to Race Condition (Different Race as Omitted Category, Standard Errors in Parentheses)

Independent Variable	Among Black Respondents	Among White Respondents
Age	0.017 (0.011)	−0.007 (0.008)
Gender (Male)	−0.026 (0.252)	−0.015 (0.215)
Income	−0.035 (0.045)	0.006 (0.036)
Partisanship	0.068 (0.069)	−0.002 (0.049)
Constant	−0.971 (0.532)	−0.234 (0.452)
Prob > Chi-Square	0.458	0.944
N	291	353

4

Compassion, Gender, and Parenthood

For much of this book, I have considered perceptions of compassion in a social vacuum. I have shown that candidates who make credible empathetic appeals are perceived as more compassionate than those who make sympathetic appeals. I have further provided evidence that commonalities such as experience, emotion, and identity drive perceptions that a candidate cares about others and is, therefore, worthy of one's vote.

Do these findings apply equally to the evaluations citizens make of all politicians or just to politicians who fit a particular archetype? And how do messaging strategies intended to boost perceptions of compassion interact with a complex information environment where messages compete with one another for attention and are filtered through the biases of a stereotyping public. Chapters 4 and 5 offer an opportunity to "zoom out" and consider how compassion interacts with other important features of American politics.

Although I have examined the intersection of candidate race and partisanship, other factors may interact with empathetic messages. In this chapter, I address how gender and parenthood can shape the way Americans view politicians of different backgrounds. Culturally, our society has most often associated the concepts of empathy, sympathy, and compassion with the nurturing role of mothers. These stereotypes may be an asset to women seeking public office during times when compassion is especially valued. Yet, as I show here, the built-in advantage women have on perceptions of compassion can also serve as a straitjacket constraining how women present themselves to the voting public. Although much is known about the ways gender stereotypes shape trait perceptions, relatively less is known about how these stereotypes constrain the ways candidates can message on matters of personal character.

In exploring the interaction of gender and compassion, I note that campaigns often face a choice in the types of traits they can champion.

Feeling Their Pain. Jared McDonald, Oxford University Press. © Oxford University Press 2024.
DOI: 10.1093/oso/9780197696897.003.0004

During times of war, strength and leadership skills may be considered more valuable than compassion. And a candidate with a history in the military may naturally want to emphasize her strength and decision-making skills, while a schoolteacher may wish to emphasize her more nurturing side. In other words, the attributes of individual candidates incentivize the types of messages campaigns employ. Yet I show that the electorate imposes other constraints, as even a woman with a military background may find herself paying a penalty when she emphasizes her leadership and foreign policy skills due to deeply engrained gender stereotypes.

With this chapter I offer two pieces of evidence related to the effect of gender and parenthood on perceptions of compassion. First, I explore how candidate gender and character-based political rhetoric intersect to shape public opinion. This approach recognizes that compassion is only one trait that candidates may choose to emphasize, and the gender of the politician may matter in such decisions. What I show is disheartening. Although women may be advantaged on matters of compassion, they are pigeon-holed in ways that men are not. Men have traditionally occupied positions of power, so there are fewer expectations about the "type" of person or leader they are supposed to be. They are assumed to be strong leaders but are not punished when conveying compassion, since there is a long tradition of men emphasizing their caring and nurturing side when seeking public office. Women are often assumed to be compassionate, but they are punished for going "against type" and emphasizing traits associated with competence and leadership rather than caring. Because these traits are associated with mas-culinity, women are perceived negatively when they emphasize them. Men, however, are rewarded for subverting gendered expectations by emphasizing compassion. This indicates they can emphasize their role as fathers and nurturers, but women cannot emphasize their role as CEOs or decision-makers as effectively.

Second, I return to the notion of empathy through commonality, exploring the degree to which men and women have the capacity to draw on their backgrounds as parents to connect with parents in the voting public. What I find here is somewhat more encouraging. Using survey data, I show that when respondents share the background of the candidate (in this case, whether they are parents), it meaningfully shapes perceptions of compas-sion. This is the case for both men and women seeking public office, meaning both men and women politicians appear to be able to effectively message around issues related to raising a family. Also consistent with the theory of empathy through commonality, I find support for the notion that men and women who identify strongly with their gender view politicians of their own gender to be more compassionate and more favorable overall.

4.1 Motherhood and Compassion

Themes of compassion and motherhood often come to the forefront of campaigns when women are seeking elected office. When Kirsten Gillibrand launched her campaign for the 2020 Democratic presidential nomination, she did so claiming that she would restore "the compassion in this country." As evidence of this, she made repeated references to her role as a mother and emphasized this by burping a baby doll she was given as a gag gift by late-night comedian Stephen Colbert. The 2020 Democratic nomination process was notable not only for the fact that six women were seeking the nomination, but also they were largely emphasizing their role as compassionate mothers in their bid to win over primary voters. As Samantha Schmidt of the *Washington Post* put it:

> In her own stump speech, Sen. Elizabeth Warren (D-Mass.) talked about potty-training her daughter in five days to meet the requirements of a daycare—with the help of three bags of M&Ms. And in a CNN town hall, Sen. Amy Klobuchar (D-Minn.) recounted how she was forced to leave a hospital just 24 hours after giving birth to her daughter, an experience that motivated the now-presidential candidate to advocate for a state law guaranteeing a 48-hour hospital stay for new moms.[1]

The salience of motherhood when women candidates seek political office spans the partisan spectrum. Whereas Democratic women wed the notion of motherhood to policy priorities like access to daycare and healthcare, Republican women use it to burnish their credentials on Republican priorities around abortion, school choice, and national security. In seeking the 2014 Oregon GOP nomination for U.S. Senate, Monica Wehby referenced her role as a mother and a pediatric neurosurgeon as qualifications for serving

---

[1] Samantha Schmidt, "Women candidates for 2020 are putting motherhood front and center," *Washington Post*, February 26, 2019.

in Congress. In an ad entitled "Trust," a mother tearfully recounted the story of how Dr. Wehby had saved her child's life, performing a surgery to correct a defect in the child's spine after other doctors had recommended terminating the pregnancy. Former congresswoman and presidential candidate Michelle Bachmann got her start in politics by founding charter schools and serving on the school's board after she grew disillusioned with the quality of public schools. As both a candidate for Congress and president, she spoke of her motivation for public service as stemming from a concern about the welfare of her children and foster children, with the quality of America's schools central to this claim.[2] And when Tennessee Senator Marsha Blackburn advocated for more stringent deterrents against illegal immigration amid a surge in border crossings in 2021, she spoke not of the threats coming from outside the country, but her empathy for those coming across who would be victimized by organized crime:

> It is so heartbreaking to me. I'm a mom, I'm a grandmom. And to see these kids and to know that there are sex trafficking, human trafficking, labor work crews, gangs that they may end up with. This is absolutely devastating. It is a humanitarian crisis. It is a drug crisis. It is an environmental crisis as well a law enforcement crisis at our border.[3]

The ways women have messaged around matters of gender and leadership have evolved since the nation's founding, and it is not the focus of this book to outline all the ways gender biases manifest and constrain messages from candidates for office. Yet, from the Mothers Against Drunk Driving organizing movement to restrict the access of alcohol, to Tipper Gore's advocacy of labeling explicit music with the Parents Music Resource Center in the mid-1980s, women's participation in politics is seemingly more welcome when it comes from a background as a compassionate nurturer interested in protecting children. As such, it is worthwhile to examine how messages of compassion, strength, and parenthood are perceived by an electorate that stereotypes on the basis of gender.

---

[2] Ryan Lizza, "Leap of faith: The making of a Republican front-runner," *The New Yorker*, August 8, 2011.

[3] Senator Marsha Blackburn Youtube Channel, "Cartels issuing wristbands to traffic children on the border," March 24, 2021.

4.2 Research on Gender and Character

Stories like those from Monica Wehby, Michelle Bachmann, and Marsha Blackburn highlight the gendered nature of compassion. Women, on the one hand, may be advantaged because voters assume women are inherently caring. Based on the analyses from previous chapters, one might suspect that women would have a built-in advantage when it comes to winning office, most especially in roles where compassion is prioritized above other qualifications. Conversely, however, citizens may also assume that women are weaker, less assertive leaders.

Social psychologists point to two dimensions of character that often differentiate men and women: communion and agency. These meta-traits embody many individual characteristics but are largely defined by whether there is a clear instrumental benefit at hand. Communion embodies personal warmth, compassion, and an ability to find common ground or consensus, where social well-being is prioritized even though there is no tangible payoff as a result. Scholars commonly view these as feminine traits (Abele 2003; Hayes 2011, 2005), suggesting a woman may be assumed to have these qualities while a man may not. Agency embodies instrumental qualities like competence, assertiveness, and decisiveness, which are associated with men (Abele et al. 2008). Although a great deal of research finds that gender stereotypes can have both positive and negative influences on election outcomes for men and women seeking office, far less is known about the ways these gender stereotypes inhibit men and women from messaging around themes of compassion and leadership.

Although gender stereotypes conceivably cut both ways, both advantaging and disadvantaging men and women depending on which traits are more valued at a given time, the majority of existing research on men and women seeking public office finds that stereotyping consistently hurts women more. Politics are traditionally viewed as the domain of men, and traits associated with leadership are viewed as having a masculine quality. Historically, women could enter the political arena, but only when a feminine perspective was needed.

Masculine qualities are considered crucial for holding elected office (Huddy and Terkildsen 1993), yet women who evoke those qualities run the risk of being seen as less feminine, breaking with traditional gender norms (Eagly and Karau 2002; Rudman 1998; Rudman et al. 2012; Stivers 2002). In her crucial work on the gender "double-bind," Kathleen Hall Jamieson

(1995) notes that women who want to be taken seriously as public leaders must demonstrate competent, strong leadership in order to succeed. Yet by conveying strength in traits traditionally associated with men, women are thus perceived as less feminine and viewed in a more negative light (see also Guy 1995; Lawrence and Rose 2010; Lawless 2004; McThomas and Tesler 2016). In this way, women pay a cost relative to men who do not face an incongruence between traditional gender roles and norms of leadership. Due to these limiting factors, recent research finds that women are only able to win at roughly the same rates as men because they are more qualified and more successful legislators than their male counterparts (Bauer 2020; Conroy 2015; Holman, Merolla, and Zechmeister 2011, 2017).

The previous example from Marsha Blackburn helps illustrate this predicament. Blackburn is speaking about issues of immigration and national security, ones in which she is at an inherent disadvantage due to women being perceived as less capable on matters of foreign policy (Hayes 2011). Yet she deftly reframes the issue as a humanitarian crisis, drawing on her experience as a mother and grandmother to express her passion for the goal of saving the children who will be drawn in to lives of crime or destitution. While some may view her rise to service in the U.S. Senate as evidence that gender biases are not that serious, the bulk of the research on gender and leadership shows that women who seek elected office must be relatively exceptional to succeed.

4.3 Gender Stereotyping and Backlash Effects

The source of the gender double-bind is thought to stem from harmful stereotypes. Citizens infer a great deal about the characteristics and values of politicians from visible characteristics such as gender (Brooks 2013; Fox and Oxley 2003; Dolan 2004, 2014; Hayes 2011; Huddy and Terkildsen 1993; Koch 2000; Lawless 2004; Sanbonmatsu 2002). Based on the gender of the politician, citizens make assumptions about ideology (Alexander and Andersen 1993; King and Matland 2003; McDermott 1998, 2005), policy expertise (Alexander and Andersen 1993; Lawless 2004), and the character of the candidate (Best and Williams 1990; Hayes 2005; McKee and Sheriffs 1957; Winter 2010).

These stereotypes matter due to the judgments citizens make when they evaluate a politician. Upon first encountering a politician, citizens begin to generate an impression of who the candidate is, what issues or groups are likely to be first and foremost in the candidate's mind, and the type of person the candidate is. Women seeking office are likely to be viewed initially as compassionate nurturers, but if they do not play into that stereotype they might be described as cold or unapproachable, descriptors seldom used for men.

Women, unlike men, are likely to be punished for not conforming to gender stereotypes about character. In particular, expectancy-violation theory (e.g., Burgoon 1993) argues that individuals are most responsive to information that runs counter to expectations. These expectations may be shaped in part by cultural values, so a society in which women are expected to behave differently from men can result in individuals who perceive a person more negatively if they subvert gender roles. Moreover, because men are more commonly in positions of power, their presence in leadership does not strike observers as unusual.

Similarly, role incongruity theory (Eagly 1987) argues that many will simply refuse to see women as "good fits" for leadership roles. Eagly and Karau (2002) argue that this stems from individuals in society believing some attribute about a particular group (e.g., women are compassionate) while simultaneously believing that this attribute is incongruent with success in a particular role (e.g., being compassionate is inconsistent with being a good leader in business or government).

Finally, implicit leadership theory (e.g., Lord et al. 2020) suggests that people hold in their minds features that separate leaders from non-leaders. Synthesizing these features into some abstract "prototype" of the ideal leader, real-world leaders are evaluated by how well they measure up against this figure (Gabora, Rosch, and Aerts 2008). Here, again, gender stereotypes create costs for women that men do not pay. If citizens use past leaders as a way of developing an impression for the perfect leader, they will be drawing from a pool of real-world examples dominated by men. Only through greater representation of women in leadership positions can this bias be resolved.

Drawing from the research on expectancy violation, role incongruity, and implicit leadership, scholars find that stereotypes create a backlash for women in leadership (e.g., DeHart-Davis et al. 2020; Rudman 1998; Rudman et al. 2012) and in society more broadly (e.g., Ridgeway 2011). Because character traits of leadership and compassion are "owned" by men and women, respectively (Hayes 2011, 2005),[4] women may be confronted with a choice

---

[4] Although perceptions of character are shaped by gender, Hayes (2011) also finds that these stereotypes have a more limited effect when partisanship is present, as partisanship becomes the dominant factor shaping perceptions of character.

when conveying messages of personal character: conform to expectations and emphasize compassion or go against type and emphasize leadership. In cases where leadership is especially valued or the woman running for office has a strong background in matters related to the military or foreign policy, the candidate may feel advantaged by messaging around themes of leadership and decision-making in high-pressure situations. Yet in doing so, she may pay a cost for not hewing to stereotypes by emphasizing compassion.

Existing research suggests that it is not only important for women in leadership to resist the temptation to go "against type" but that they also may be particularly vulnerable to criticism that undermines their perceived strength on compassion. Examining the impact of negative campaigning and political scandals, Cassese and Holman (2018) provide evidence that women suffer the harshest punishment from voters when they are attacked in ways that undermine evaluations of character most closely associated with femininity. Scandals puncture the perceived strength women have in morality judgements (e.g., Barnes, Beaulieu, and Saxton 2020; Zemojtel-Piotrowska et al. 2017), undercutting an important strength women have over men in electoral competitions. Taken together, it suggests that women who run for office are put in a position of "do no harm." Voters may assume that women are compassionate, so running on themes of compassion should do little to enhance electoral prospects. Yet running on leadership risks a backlash and negative personal stories may be especially damaging, leaving compassion as the dominant strategy for women candidates.

In sum, men and women seeking public office face pressures to conform to different standards. A woman who violates a norm or stereotype suffers in ways that a man does not. Stated formally, I hypothesize the following:

H5. Messages related to leadership will result in lower favorability for women seeking elected office when compared to messages related to compassion or no trait at all.

Should we also expect to see men who go against type pay a penalty? In other words, might it have been true that a candidate like Bill Clinton was perceived more negatively because he chose to emphasize compassion in his campaigns for the presidency rather than strong leadership? Undoubtedly, candidates with the amount of attention Bill Clinton received will make the case that they are both strong *and* compassionate leaders, but should we expect to see a man pay a penalty when he emphasizes his compassion? In contrast to my expectations about women, here I expect that there may be a bonus for men who subvert gender stereotypes.

The literature I have reviewed on the source of backlash effects for women in leadership notes that the backlash is predicated on a threat to status quo power structures. Namely, Rudman et al. (2012) show that backlash is moderated by the desire to preserve the existing gender hierarchy. Although women entering politics are, by their very existence in an electoral contest, posing a threat to the gender hierarchy, they do so especially if they do not emphasize traditionally feminine traits as their qualification to serve. Men, however, have long dominated politics, with many of them emphasizing compassion. Neither Bill Clinton's brand of "I feel your pain" politics nor George W. Bush's "compassionate conservatism" posed serious threats to existing gender hierarchies and therefore were unlikely to incur a backlash.

Moreover, there is good reason to believe men, unlike women, will benefit for going against type. Both leadership and compassion are considered positive qualities in a candidate for elected office (e.g., Kinder 1986). Voters using gender stereotypes to inform their choices may assume that a man is already a strong, decisive leader. By conveying compassion, he will be shoring up one area in which he may have been perceived to be weak. I therefore hypothesize the following:

> H6. *Messages related to compassion will result in higher favorability for men seeking elected office when compared to messages related to leadership or no trait at all.*

4.4 Experimental Evidence on Penalties for Going Against Type

In order to assess whether citizens penalize women candidates relative to male candidates for evoking "masculine" character traits, I rely on a survey experiment conducted February 25–28, 2020, on a sample of 807 American adults who volunteered to take the survey through Amazon's Mechanical Turk (MTurk).

4.4.1 Design

Similar to the experiments described in Chapter 3, this 2x3 experiment employs vignettes that vary the candidate's gender and the character trait they are evoking (compassion, leadership, no trait).[5] Each respondent reads a block of text purporting to be an excerpt from a news article. Regardless of the experimental condition to which the respondent is assigned, all participants read about a candidate making a run for the U.S. House of Representatives (named David/Debbie Allen). In the control, respondents only read basic background information on the candidate. In the treatment conditions, Allen evokes a character trait as the motivating factor for their run. In the compassion condition, Allen claims, "I am running for Congress because I care about the people of this district." Conversely, in the leadership condition, Allen asserts, "I'm running for Congress because I know how to lead." By varying the gender of the candidate conveying the message, I can examine how women and men seeking public office are viewed when they emphasize character traits that have traditionally gendered connotations. The manipulations are subtle to maintain comparability across conditions. As previously demonstrated, compassionate appeals are more effective when there is an empathetic connection that lends credibility to the claim. Yet this approach would introduce potential confounds, so the treatments are left as relatively superficial claims of caring or leadership.

After reading the vignettes to which they are assigned, respondents are then asked to answer several questions about the candidate mentioned in the story. I examine three key dependent variables: (1) perceptions of candidate compassion, (2) perceptions of candidate leadership, and (3) overall favorability.[6] All items use 5-point Likert scales that are recoded from 0 to 1 for purposes of analysis.[7]

---

[5] Full research design featuring vignettes and survey items can be found in the appendix to this chapter.

[6] In the survey flow, favorability was asked first to avoid contrast effects (Schwarz and Bless 1992). The order of perceptions of compassion, leadership, and knowledge was randomized.

[7] It is possible the treatments are not solely influencing perceptions of compassion and leadership (and therefore favorability) but are instead generating an overall positive valence toward the candidates. This would be an important confound to the experimental findings (Dafoe Zhang, and Caughey 2018). To address this, I include an additional item designed as a placebo. I asked respondents to rate how knowledgeable they perceived the candidate to be, as neither treatment was intended to significantly influence perceptions of candidate knowledgeability. I then employed a repeated-measures approach to examine whether the compassion and leadership treatments had a statistically distinguishable effect on their respective outcomes relative to perceptions of knowledge. Results from the repeated-measures analysis show that the compassion and leadership treatments did, in fact, have statistically significant and distinguishable effects on perceptions of compassion and leadership, respectively, that did not transfer to perceptions of knowledge. Results are in the appendix to this chapter.

4.4.2   Results

I begin by assessing whether men and women seeking to convey compassion and leadership are viewed better on those character traits and whether those perceptions translate into higher overall evaluations (Figure 4.1). Figure 4.1A reveals that women and men are both perceived as significantly more compassionate when they make claims of caring about the people they seek to represent ($p<0.01$).[8] Though intuitive, it is noteworthy that *both* men and women are perceived as relatively more compassionate when they convey messages of caring. Compassion is a trait normally associated with women, but men appear to be able to overcome any skepticism on this trait with relative ease. Simply claiming to care significantly increases respondents' perceptions that the person described in the story cares about people like them. Not surprisingly, when the candidates convey messages related to leadership, they do not increase the perception that the candidates are more compassionate.

Figure 4.1B shows that rewards for going against type do not extend to women. While men who convey messages about strong leadership receive a significant boost in these perceptions ($p<0.01$), women who convey the same messages are not perceived to have stronger leadership qualities. These results show that women seeking office face a deeply skeptical public; one not willing to take female candidates at their word when they say they are strong leaders.

Although perceptions of candidate character are illustrative, overall favorability should be the most consequential evaluation for a candidate in an election (e.g., Croco, Hanmer, and McDonald 2020). Here the results are most stark. When the candidates conform to expectations based on gender stereotypes, there is little overall movement. Women who convey caring and men who convey leadership see positive movement in terms of general favorability, but effects are small and not statistically significant. These traits are expected from the politicians, based on candidate gender, so they do little to alter general evaluations.

When women and men go against type, however, the results are the polar opposite. For men, there is a greater than 9-percentage-point increase in favorability, which is statistically significant at conventional levels ($p<0.01$).

---

[8] I.e., $p<0.05$ for the female candidate condition, $p<0.01$ for the male candidate condition.

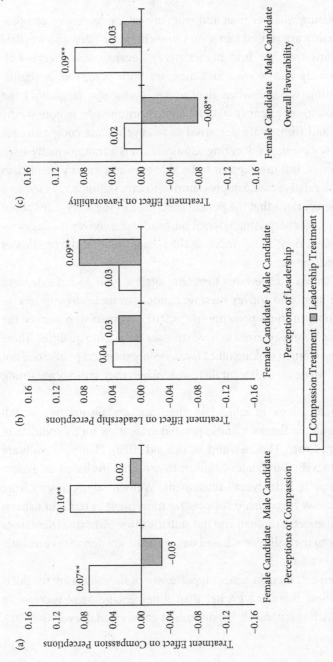

Figure 4.1 Treatment Effects for All Possible Combinations of Treatments.

** Effects are statistically significant at $p<0.01$

Note: Effect sizes are assessed relative to the control condition in which neither compassion nor leadership was evoked.

In comparison, women who seek to convey their strong leadership skills not only fail to generate the perception that they are stronger leaders but also see a statistically significant *drop* in overall favorability by nearly 8 percentage points ($p<0.05$).

The treatment effects are not substantially moderated by the gender of the respondent. Although one might easily imagine that men, more than women, would punish female candidates for going against type, the data do not support that conclusion. For example, I find that women view female candidates less favorably by roughly 8.3 percentage points when they invoke the trait of leadership, but they view the male candidates roughly 8.7 percentage points more favorably when they invoke compassion. Men in the sample are similar, punishing female candidates by roughly 7.2 percentage points on favorability when they invoke leadership and rewarding male candidates who invoke compassion by 9.8 percentage points (full results by gender of the respondent are located in table A4.1 of the appendix to this chapter).[9] The tendency to use gender stereotypes to punish female candidates who go against type, it appears, is equally strong among men and women.

The findings clearly show that women and men are on very different playing fields. Candidates face vastly different incentive structures based solely on their gender when trying to cultivate a positive public image. While compassion is conventionally viewed as a feminine quality, men benefit greatly by showing they are not simply strong leaders but also caring ones. Women, conversely, face a harsh backlash. Strong leadership skills are expected of politicians, yet when women seek to run on leadership they suffer in the public eye. As a result, women are under pressure to adopt a "do no harm" strategy in positions of political power, as the woman who conveys compassion performs no better than the control, and the woman who conveys strong leadership is perceived more negatively.

4.5 Commonalities Through Gender and Parenthood

The previous experiment shows that, although women may be assumed to be compassionate, Americans are often less receptive when women go against

---

[9] These sorts of subsample analyses should be interpreted with some caution. With roughly 800 respondents in these analyses, there is insufficient power to detect moderation effects. With Table A4.1 in the appendix, I wish to illustrate that the substantive results do not appear driven by men or women individually and that trends that exist for one category persist for the other.

gender stereotypes by emphasizing their talents as strong leaders. That experiment simply compared candidates who emphasized one trait relative to another but did not examine the ability of specific commonalities to shape perceptions of compassion across gender type. There remains the question, then, of whether salient identities and experiences that are often linked to gender shape how compassionate appeals are received by the masses.

In campaign settings, candidates often discuss their backgrounds as mothers and fathers to connect with voters who are themselves parents or have concerns about the environment in which children are being raised. These types of appeals have been used overwhelmingly by women, which is unsurprising given the penalties women face for emphasizing other characteristics. When candidates seek to connect with voters on matters related to parenthood, they can make empathetic appeals that tap both experience (that of raising a child) and identity (fatherhood or motherhood). Do these types of appeals resonate with the public as the theory of empathy through commonality would anticipate? And do gender biases constrain the types of messages candidates can convey about parenthood? To explore this, I turn to an additional study conducted April 14–15, 2022, on a sample of 1,707 American adults who volunteered to take a series of survey experiments through the platform Lucid.[10]

4.5.1 Design

Gender identity should be in important moderator of the effect of a shared gender between the respondent and the politician on perceptions of compassion.[11] As the theory of empathy through commonality would suggest, only those who view their gender identity as important to defining "people like me" should differentiate greatly between men and women seeking elected office.

To assess this, the study asked all respondents to provide their gender and answer a four-item battery of questions intended to measure gender social identity (developed by Huddy, Mason, and Aaroe 2015). These items were

---

[10] Some analyses have smaller samples due to the exclusion of respondents who failed attention checks.
[11] Full research design featuring vignettes and survey items can be found in the appendix to this chapter.

used to create an index ranging from 0 to 1 for gender identity. For ease of interpretation, respondents were categorized as being either high or low in gender identity based on whether they were above or below the mean value for the sample.[12]

The experiment employs a 2×2 vignette design, varying the gender of candidate and whether the candidate is making an empathetic appeal for parents' votes or whether they are making a sympathetic claim of caring about the concerns of parents (without a claim of being a parent themselves).[13] Respondents again read a news story describing either David or Debbie Allen's candidacy for Congress. In the sympathetic, no parenthood appeal, Allen asserts that they are running because they care about parents and the children of the district. They state, "I've talked to countless [fathers/mothers] afraid about what the future holds for their children." In the empathetic, parenthood appeal, Allen instead states, "I'm a father who is afraid about what the future holds for my children" (full vignettes can be found in the appendix to this chapter).

Two features of the experiment merit special attention. First, the manipulations were relatively minor by necessity to capture the sympathy/empathy distinction developed in Chapter 3. Parents should generally like these candidates regardless of the manipulation, since in all conditions there is at least a clear claim of caring about parents. Yet the theory I have laid out expects that parents should still perceive the candidate who makes explicit mention of his or her *own* kids to be somewhat more compassionate than a candidate who simply claims to care about children. Second, although the conditions in which Allen is a parent are traditionally "empathetic," this may not be true for all respondents. For example, a respondent who does not have kids would lack this commonality with the politician. Instead, the theory of empathy through commonality would suggest that respondents without kids would prefer the candidate who simply claims to care about parents and kids over the one who has kids. For that reason, I do not refer to these conditions as "sympathy" and "empathy" conditions but rather as "no kids" or "kids" conditions, respectively, allowing me to examine what happens when the respondent and the politician share this commonality.

---

[12] Conclusions do not change if analyses are run using the continuous measure of gender identity.

[13] The experiment also randomized the partisanship of the politician, though this feature is not a part of the analysis that follows.

In the analysis that follows, I examine the two outcomes of primary interest: (1) perceptions of candidate compassion, and (2) overall favorability. Consistent with prior analyses, these 5-point Likert scales were recoded from 0 to 1 for purposes of analysis.

4.5.2   Results

Figures 4.2A and 4.2B show mean levels of perceptions of compassion and favorability across the "no kids" and "kids" conditions. These differences are shown separately for respondents who are not parents and for respondents who are parents. First, I find that, regardless of condition, individuals with kids perceive the politician described in the vignette to be more compassionate and more favorable. This is unsurprising, since in all conditions the politician is making an explicit appeal to the parents of the congressional district. It is also consistent with the finding in Chapter 3 that politicians who cannot make a credible empathetic appeal are incentivized to make a sympathetic appeal.

But does parenthood act as an important commonality through which Americans perceive compassion? In Chapter 3, I showed that relatively universal empathetic claims of having lived a humble life are more attractive to a broad swath of Americans than simply claiming to care about working-class Americans. With the more specific claim of parenthood, I similarly find that experiential bonds shape perceptions of compassion. Among respondents without children, the politician who *lacks* children is perceived as being slightly more compassionate, by a margin of roughly 3 points compared to the candidate who makes the explicit parenthood appeal (Figure 4.2A). For respondents who are parents, the relationship is reversed. They view the politicians who are parents as more compassionate by roughly 3 points when there is the common bond of parenthood. Although these differences are modest, taken together they suggest there is a roughly 6-point swing in terms of perceptions of compassion depending on the match or mismatch of the experiential bond of parenthood.

The results on favorability are largely consistent with the findings on perceptions of compassion (Figure 4.2B), though the differences are even smaller and in this case no longer statistically significant.

Importantly, however, I do not find evidence that the gender of the candidate played an important role in moderating these relationships.

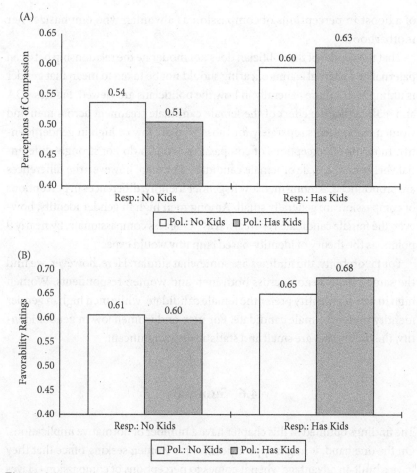

Figure 4.2

(A) Perceptions of Compassion Across the Parenthood Status of the Politician and Respondent

Note: The difference-in-difference across respondents without kids and respondents with kids is statistically significant at conventional levels (*p*<0.05).

(B) Favorability Across the Parenthood Status of the Politician and Respondent

Note: The difference-in-difference across respondents without kids and respondents with kids is not statistically significant at conventional levels.

Respondents who are parents generally view politicians who are parents as more compassionate, regardless of whether that politician is a man or a woman. As the first study in this chapter suggested, men are not constrained on matters of compassion. A man who makes a claim of caring and ties it back to his experiences as a father receives just as much of a boost in perceptions of compassion as a woman who emphasizes her motherhood.

That the gender of the politician does not moderate the relationship between paternal or maternal claims of caring should not be taken to mean that gender is unimportant more generally in how the politicians are viewed. Figures 4.3A and 4.3B depict the effect of the female candidate treatment across men and women respondents separately for those who are low or high in gender identity. In terms of perceptions of compassion, women do not strongly differentiate between the male or female candidate. For men, however, the differences are pronounced. Among men low in gender identity, differences in perceptions of compassion are generally small. Among men high in gender identity, however, the female candidate is perceived as being less compassionate, by nearly 9 points, as the theory of identity-based empathy would expect.

For favorability, the findings are somewhat similar. Here, however, we find the same phenomenon across both men and women respondents. Women high in gender identity prefer the female candidate, while men high in gender identity prefer the male candidate. For men and women low in gender identity, the differences are small and statistically insignificant.

4.6 Summary

The findings outlined in this chapter have a number of normative implications. On the one hand, it might appear positive for women seeking office that they have a built-in advantage when it comes to perceptions of compassion (Hayes 2011). This is a trait I have argued is not only important but also often decisive in campaigns. Yet this benefit comes with a tremendous number of strings attached. Women may be viewed as compassionate, but they are punished for seeking to convince voters that they have other positive traits beyond compassion. Men, on the other hand, benefit from conveying both compassion and strong leadership traits, whereas women are penalized for conveying strong leadership and receive no added benefit in running on compassion. Similarly, I have found that parenthood can be a strong commonality that links candidates and citizens, shaping perceptions of compassion for both mothers and fathers seeking election. Here, both men and women were perceived similarly when campaigning around fatherhood/motherhood, suggesting men are not at an inherent disadvantage when conveying traditionally feminine messages.

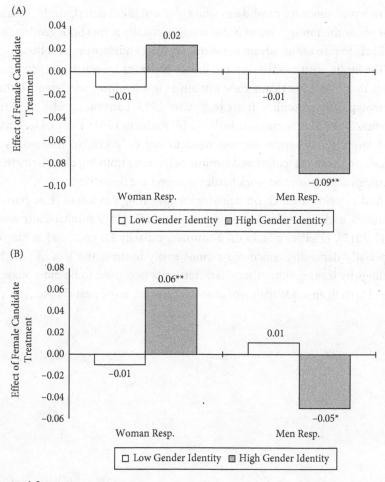

Figure 4.3

(A) Effect of Female Treatment on Perceptions of Compassion for Women and Men Respondents by Levels of Gender Identity

**Effects are statistically significant at $p<0.01$

(B) Effect of Female Treatment on Favorability for Women and Men Respondents by Levels of Gender Identity

*Effects are statistically significant at $p<0.05$

**Effects are statistically significant at $p<0.01$

Yet even though the gender of the politician does not interact with the messaging strategy, gender remains an important determinant of perceptions of compassion and public approval. Men and women high in gender identity show a preference for candidates who represent them descriptively. Because this phenomenon appears to occur roughly equally across both genders, it is unlikely to provide an advantage to one type of candidate over another.

The findings on compassion and leadership traits are consistent with other work that finds Americans view women as less feminine for demonstrating stereotypically masculine traits (e.g., Guy 1995; Lawrence and Rose 2010; Lawless 2004; McThomas and Tesler 2016; Rudman 1998). Dolan, Deckman, and Swers (2019) argue women need to not only present themselves as possessing both masculine and feminine character traits but also clarify their ideological position and work harder to overcome these barriers.

And as prior research on negative campaigning has found (e.g., Barnes, Beaulieu, and Saxton 2020; Cassese and Holman 2018; Zemojtel-Piotrowska et al. 2017), negative attacks on a woman's capacity for compassion may be especially damaging, since she cannot easily buttress the loss of positive feelings by leaning into other character traits perceived to be more masculine. I turn to an examination of character attacks in the next chapter.

Appendix: Survey Instruments and Results

2020 Amazon Mechanical Turk Study Design

Q1

Please randomly assign all respondents into six conditions.

EXPERIMENTAL CONDITIONS

1 Man Control
2 Man Cares
3 Man Leader
4 Woman Control
5 Woman Cares
6 Woman Leader

Introduction:

On the next page, you will read about a candidate for Congress in the upcoming election. Please read the description carefully and respond to the questions that follow.

Q1a

Please display to those who were assigned to Condition 1 in Q1.

Allen Announces Bid for Congress

David Allen, a local grocery store owner, is running for a seat in the U.S. House of Representatives as a Democrat. He is sixty-eight years old and has two children with his wife of forty years. While he has long been a prominent citizen in his community and active in local politics, this is the first time he has run for Congress. In his first public speech since filing to run for office, Allen told the crowd, "I am asking each and every one of you for your vote this upcoming November election."

David Allen

Q1b

Please display to those who were assigned to Condition 2 in Q1.

Allen Announces Bid for Congress, Touts Compassion

David Allen, a local grocery store owner, is running for a seat in the U.S. House of Representatives as a Democrat. He is sixty-eight years old and has two children with his wife of forty years. While he has long been a prominent citizen in his community and active in local politics, this is the first time he has run for Congress. In his first public speech since filing to run for office, Allen said that what was missing in Congress was a sense of compassion. Allen told the crowd, "I'm running for Congress because I care about the people of this district. I am asking each and every one of you for your vote this upcoming November election."

Q1c

Please display to those who were assigned to Condition 3 in Q1.

Allen Announces Bid for Congress, Touts Leadership

David Allen, a local grocery store owner, is running for a seat in the U.S. House of Representatives as a Democrat. He is sixty-eight years old and has two children with his wife of forty years. While he has long been a prominent citizen in his community and active in local politics, this is the first time he has run for Congress. In his first public speech since filing to run for office, Allen said that what was missing in Congress was strong leadership. Allen told the crowd, "I'm for Congress because I know how to lead. I am asking each and every one of you for your vote this upcoming November election."

Q1d

Please display to those who were assigned to Condition 4 in Q1.

Allen Announces Bid for Congress

Debbie Allen, a local grocery store owner, is running for a seat in the U.S. House of Representatives as a Democrat. She is sixty-eight years old and has two children with her husband of forty years. While she has long been a prominent citizen in her community and active in local politics, this is the first time she has run for Congress. In her first public speech since filing to run for office, Allen told the crowd, "I

Debbie Allen

am asking each and every one of you for your vote this upcoming November election."

Q1e

Please display to those who were assigned to Condition 5 in Q1.

Allen Announces Bid for Congress, Touts Compassion

Debbie Allen, a local grocery store owner, is running for a seat in the U.S. House of Representatives as a Democrat. She is sixty-eight years old and has two children with her husband of forty years. While she has long been a prominent citizen in her community and active in local politics, this is the first time she has run for Congress. In her first public speech since filing to run for office, Allen said that what was missing in Congress was a sense of compassion. Allen told the crowd, "I'm running for Congress because I care about the people of this district. I am asking each and every one of you for your vote this upcoming November election."

Q1f

Please display to those who were assigned to Condition 6 in Q1.

Allen Announces Bid for Congress, Touts Leadership

Debbie Allen, a local grocery store owner, is running for a seat in the U.S. House of Representatives as a Democrat. She is sixty-eight years old and has two children with her husband of forty years. While she has long been a prominent citizen in her community and active in local politics, this is the first time she has run for Congress. In her first public speech since filing to run for office, Allen said that what was missing in Congress was strong leadership. Allen told the crowd, "I'm for Congress because I know how to lead. I am asking each and every one of you for your vote this upcoming November election."

Q2

SINGLE CHOICE

Overall, how favorable or unfavorable is your impression of David/ Debbie Allen?

1 Strongly Unfavorable
2 Somewhat Unfavorable
3 Somewhat Favorable
4 Strongly Favorable

Q3

Randomize order of Q3 and Q4.

SINGLE CHOICE

In your opinion, does the phrase, "(s)he really cares about people like you"
describe David/Debbie Allen

1 Very poorly
2 Somewhat poorly
3 Neither poorly nor well
4 Somewhat well
5 Very well

Q4

Randomize order of Q3 and Q4.

SINGLE CHOICE

In your opinion, does the phrase, "(s)he provides strong leadership" describe
David/Debbie Allen

1 Very poorly
2 Somewhat poorly
3 Neither poorly nor well
4 Somewhat well
5 Very well

Q4

Randomize order of Q3 and Q4.

SINGLE CHOICE

In your opinion, does the phrase, "(s)he is knowledgeable" describe David/
Debbie Allen

1 Very poorly
2 Somewhat poorly

3 Neither poorly nor well
4 Somewhat well
5 Very well

Results

Table A4.1 Treatment Effects by Gender of the Respondent (OLS Regression, Control Is Omitted Category, Standard Errors in Parentheses)

		Women Respondents		Men Respondents	
		Female Candidate	Male Candidate	Female Candidate	Male Candidate
Perceptions of Compassion	Compassion Treatment Effect	0.052 (0.047)	0.122** (0.041)	0.090* (0.042)	0.083* (0.041)
	Leadership Treatment Effect	−0.065 (0.051)	−0.025 (0.041)	0.002 (0.041)	0.048 (0.042)
	Constant (Control Condition)	0.656** (0.033)	0.579** (0.029)	0.569** (0.030)	0.545** (0.029)
Perceptions of Leadership	Compassion Treatment Effect	0.016 (0.048)	0.002 (0.044)	0.058 (0.038)	0.054 (0.042)
	Leadership Treatment Effect	0.023 (0.051)	0.056 (0.044)	0.047 (0.037)	0.111** (0.043)
	Constant (Control Condition)	0.612** (0.033)	0.627** (0.031)	0.533** (0.027)	0.549** (0.030)
Overall Favorability	Compassion Treatment Effect	0.011 (0.048)	0.087* (0.038)	0.033 (0.038)	0.098** (0.035)
	Leadership Treatment Effect	−0.083 (0.052)	−0.005 (0.038)	−0.072* (0.038)	0.052 (0.036)
	Constant (Control Condition)	0.674** (0.034)	0.643** (0.027)	0.648** (0.027)	0.588 (0.025)
N		151	185	241	230

*Indicates significant at $p<0.05$ (one-tailed test)
**Indicates significant at $p<0.01$ (one-tailed test)

Table A4.2 Treatment Effects Including Interaction with Gender of Respondent (OLS Regression, Control Is Omitted Category, Standard Errors in Parentheses)

Independent Variable	Perceptions of Compassion		Perceptions of Leadership		Favorability	
	Male Politician	Female Politician	Male Politician	Female Politician	Male Politician	Female Politician
Compassion Treatment	0.122** (0.044)	0.052 (0.049)	0.002 (0.046)	0.016 (0.046)	0.087* (0.039)	0.011 (0.047)
Leadership Treatment	−0.025 (0.044)	−0.065 (0.053)	0.056 (0.046)	0.023 (0.050)	−0.005 (0.039)	−0.083* (0.050)
Respondent Gender (Male)	−0.034 (0.042)	−0.087* (0.045)	−0.078* (0.045)	−0.079* (0.045)	−0.055 (0.037)	−0.026 (0.043)
Male * Compassion Treatment	−0.039 (0.059)	0.038 (0.064)	0.052 (0.061)	0.042 (0.060)	0.011 (0.052)	0.022 (0.061)
Male * Leadership Treatment	0.073 (0.059)	0.066 (0.066)	0.055 (0.062)	0.024 (0.063)	0.058 (0.053)	0.011 (0.063)
Constant	0.579** (0.031)	0.656** (0.034)	0.627** (0.032)	0.612** (0.032)	0.643** (0.027)	0.674** (0.033)
Prob>F	0.003	0.007	0.037	0.191	0.005	0.029
N	415	392	415	391	415	392

*Indicates significant at $p<0.05$ (one-tailed test)

**Indicates significant at $p<0.01$ (one-tailed test)

Table A4.3 Repeated Measures Fixed-Effects Model Using Placebo Beliefs
Outcome (Clustered Standard Errors, Control Is Omitted Category)

Independent Variable	Model 1 Compassion	Model 2 Leadership
Compassion Treatment	0.034 (0.022)	0.034 (0.022)
Leadership Treatment	0.004 (0.022)	0.004 (0.022)
Dummy (1=Leadership, 0=Placebo)	0.006 (0.016)	−0.002 (0.014)
Compassion Treatment * Leadership Observation	0.053* (0.022)	0.001 (0.019)
Leadership Treatment * Leadership Observation	−0.010 (0.022)	0.055** (0.019)
Constant	0.577** (0.015)	0.577** (0.015)
Prob>Chi-Square	0.000	0.002
N	1,614	1,613
No. of Clusters	807	807

*Indicates significant at $p<0.05$ (one-tailed test)
**Indicates significant at $p<0.01$ (one-tailed test)

Table A4.4 OLS Regression Predicting Outcomes by Treatments and Covariates

Independent Variable	Model 1 Compassion	Model 2 Leadership	Model 3 Favorability
Compassion Treatment	0.106**	0.035	0.100**
	(0.029)	(0.029)	(0.026)
Leadership Treatment	0.017	0.088**	0.026
	(0.030)	(0.029)	(0.026)
Female Treatment	0.055+	−0.008	0.057*
	(0.030)	(0.030)	(0.027)
Compassion * Female Treatments	−0.040	−0.000	−0.081*
	(0.042)	(0.042)	(0.037)
Leadership * Female Treatments	−0.053	−0.064	−0.116**
	(0.043)	(0.042)	(0.038)
Male Respondent	−0.036*	−0.050**	−0.024
	(0.018)	(0.018)	(0.016)
White Respondent	−0.079**	−0.082**	−0.098**
	(0.001)	(0.021)	(0.019)
Age	−0.001	−0.001+	−0.002**
	(0.001)	(0.001)	(0.001)
Education	0.022**	0.015*	0.024**
	(0.007)	(0.007)	(0.007)
Family Income	−0.020+	−0.027*	−0.029**
	(0.012)	(0.012)	(0.011)
Partisanship (1=Strong Democrat, 7=Strong Republican)	−0.012	−0.010*	−0.018**
	(0.004)	(0.004)	(0.003)
Constant	0.605**	0.691	0.709**
	(0.059)	(0.059)	(0.052)
Prob>F	0.000	0.000	0.000
N	807	807	807

+Indicates significant at $p<0.1$ (two-tailed test)

*Indicates significant at $p<0.05$ (two-tailed test)

**Indicates significant at $p<0.01$ (two-tailed test)

Table A4.5 Sample Demographic Balance Across Experimental Conditions

	Man-Control	Man-Compassion	Man-Leadership	Woman-Control	Woman-Compassion	Woman-Leadership
White	70%	74%	79%	83%	74%	73%
Male	55%	56%	56%	58%	60%	67%
Mean Age	37	37	37	36	39	35
College Educated	69%	67%	64%	69%	76%	65%
Income over $50k	54%	48%	50%	50%	47%	57%
Democrat	54%	56%	66%	56%	53%	55%
Republican	36%	36%	28%	33%	40%	32%
N	140	140	135	132	134	126

2022 Lucid Study Design

Pre-Treatment Questions

PT1

SINGLE CHOICE

Please select your gender.

  1 Man
  2 Woman
  3 Other

PT2

SINGLE CHOICE

How important is being a man/woman to you?

  1 Not important at all
  2 Not very important
  3 Very important
  4 Extremely important

PT3

SINGLE CHOICE

How well does the term "man"/"woman" describe you?

  1 Not at all
  2 Not very well
  3 Very well
  4 Extremely well

PT4

SINGLE CHOICE

When talking about men/women, how often do you use "we" instead of "they"?

  1 Never
  2 Rarely
  3 Some of the time
  4 Most of the time
  5 All of the time

PT5

SINGLE CHOICE

To what extent does being a man/woman make you feel important?

1 Not at all
2 Very little
3 Somewhat
4 A great deal

PT6

Single Choice

How many children do you have?

1 0
2 1
3 2
4 3
5 4 or more

Q1

Please randomly assign all respondents into six conditions.

EXPERIMENTAL CONDITIONS

1 No Kids - Man
2 Kids - Man
3 No Kids - Woman
4 Kids - Woman

Introduction:

On the next page, you will read about a candidate for Congress in the upcoming election. Please read the description carefully and respond to the questions that follow.

Q1a

Please display to those who were assigned to Condition 1 in Q1.

"I Care About Dads": Allen Announces Candidacy for Congress, Says He Will Fight for Area Parents and Kids

David Allen, a member of the city commission, is running for a seat in the U.S. House of Representatives as a [Democrat/Republican]. While he has long been active in local politics, this is the first time he has run for Congress. In his first public speech since filing to run for office, Allen said he was running to make life better for the district's children. "I've talked to countless fathers afraid about what the future holds for their children. I'm running because I care about the kids of this district and am willing to fight for them when I get to Washington."

David Allen

Q1b

Please display to those who were assigned to Condition 2 in Q1.

"I'm a Dad": Allen Announces Candidacy for Congress, Says He Will Fight for Area Parents and Kids

David Allen, a member of the city commission, is running for a seat in the U.S. House of Representatives as a [Democrat/Republican]. While he has long been active in local politics, this is the first time he has run for Congress. In his first public speech since filing to run for office, Allen said he was running to make life better for his own children. "I'm a father who is afraid about what the future holds for my children. I'm running because I care about my kids and am willing to fight for them when I get to Washington."

Q1c

Please display to those who were assigned to Condition 3 in Q1.

"I Care About Moms": Allen Announces Candidacy for Congress, Says She Will Fight for Area Parents and Kids

Debbie Allen, a member of the city commission, is running for a seat in the U.S. House of Representatives as a [Democrat/Republican]. While she has long been active in local politics, this is the first time she has run for Congress. In her first public speech since filing to run for office, Allen said she was running to make life better for the district's children. "I've talked to countless mothers afraid about what the future holds for their children. I'm running because I care about the kids of this district and am willing to fight for them when I get to Washington."

Debbie Allen

Q1d

Please display to those who were assigned to Condition 4 in Q1.

"I'm a Mom": Allen Announces Candidacy for Congress, Says She Will Fight for Area Parents and Kids

Debbie Allen, a member of the city commission, is running for a seat in the U.S. House of Representatives as a [Democrat/Republican]. While she has long been active in local politics, this is the first time she has run for Congress. In her first public speech since filing to run for office, Allen said she was running to make life better for her own children. "I'm a mother who is afraid about what the future holds for my children. I'm running because I care about my kids and am willing to fight for them when I get to Washington."

Q2

SINGLE CHOICE

Overall, how favorable or unfavorable is your impression of David/
Debbie Allen?

1 Strongly Unfavorable
2 Somewhat Unfavorable
3 Somewhat Favorable
4 Strongly Favorable

Q3

Randomize order of Q3 and Q4

SINGLE CHOICE

In your opinion, does the phrase, "(s)he really cares about people like you"
describe David/Debbie Allen

1 Very poorly
2 Somewhat poorly
3 Neither poorly nor well
4 Somewhat well
5 Very well

Q4

SINGLE CHOICE

In your opinion, does the phrase, "(s)he provides strong leadership" describe
David/Debbie Allen

1 Very poorly
2 Somewhat poorly
3 Neither poorly nor well
4 Somewhat well
5 Very well

Results

Table A4.6 OLS Regression Predicting Outcomes by Interaction of Respondent and Candidate Parenthood Status

Independent Variable	Perceptions of Compassion	Favorability
Parent Treatment	−0.032	−0.011
	(0.026)	(0.025)
Respondent Parenthood	0.058*	0.043*
	(0.025)	(0.024)
Treatment * Parenthood	0.064*	0.045
	(0.035)	(0.032)
Constant	0.537**	0.606**
	(0.020)	(0.018)
Prob>F	0.000	0.000
N	1,053	1,053

*Indicates significant at $p<0.05$ (one-tailed test)
**Indicates significant at $p<0.01$ (one-tailed test)

Table A4.7 OLS Regression Predicting Perceptions of Compassion Using Female Treatment, by Gender and Gender Identity

Independent Variable	Female Respondents		Male Respondents	
	Low Gender ID	High Gender ID	Low Gender ID	High Gender ID
Female Treatment	−0.013	0.023	−0.014	−0.088**
	(0.023)	(0.025)	(0.026)	(0.030)
Constant	0.541**	0.625**	0.531**	0.688**
	(0.017)	(0.018)	(0.017)	(0.019)
Prob>F	0.567	0.345	0.589	0.003
N	444	460	414	389

**Indicates significant at $p<0.01$ (one-tailed test)

Table A4.8 OLS Regression Predicting Favorability Using Female Treatment, by Gender and Gender Identity

Independent Variable	Female Respondents		Male Respondents	
	Low Gender ID	High Gender ID	Low Gender ID	High Gender ID
Female Treatment	−0.010	0.062**	0.011	−0.050*
	(0.021)	(0.022)	(0.025)	(0.029)
Constant	0.616**	0.667**	0.582**	0.696**
	(0.015)	(0.016)	(0.017)	(0.019)
Prob>F	0.640	0.005	0.665	0.080
N	445	461	413	387

*Indicates significant at $p<0.05$ (one-tailed test)

**Indicates significant at $p<0.01$ (one-tailed test)

5

The Dark Side of Compassion

In a 2015 ad entitled "Family Strong," Hillary Clinton detailed her mother's mistreatment as a child, discussing how her mother had been abandoned by her parents when she was only eight years old. In recalling this story, Clinton tried to tie her family history to her presidential campaign's broad message about social justice and caring for America's kids. "My mom's life and what she went through are big reasons why standing up for kids and families became such a big part of my life."[1] The *Washington Post*'s Chris Cillizza noted that these ads were likely a response to Clinton's falling favorability ratings,[2] making it necessary for the Clinton campaign to reintroduce their candidate to the primary voting electorate as a sincere and relatable person.

Later that same month, the *New York Times* reported that Hillary Clinton earned $13.17 million in speaking fees from the banking industry, including Wall Street firms such as Goldman Sachs. In subsequent months, Clinton's primary opponent, Vermont Senator Bernie Sanders, repeatedly mentioned these speaking fees, claiming to have "doubts about people receiving large amounts of money from Wall Street."[3]

How are these two stories related? In this chapter, I argue that they are two sides of the same coin. Candidates try to portray themselves as compassionate individuals. They lean into personal stories and those of close friends and family to convince voters that they are trustworthy and will fight for ordinary Americans once in office. Yet these messages do not occur in a vacuum. At the same time that Hillary Clinton sought to leverage her mother's childhood experiences as evidence of her motivation to fight for American families, political opponents were using her history of speeches to Wall Street firms many blamed for the 2008 economic crash as reason to doubt her authenticity and willingness to fight for the poor and middle classes. As I have noted throughout this book, the commonalities I discuss must be relevant

[1] Hillary Clinton Campaign ad, "Family Strong." August 2, 2015.
[2] Chris Cillizza, "Hillary Clinton's new ads are good. But it's remarkable that she has to run them," *Washington Post*, August 3, 2015.
[3] "Sanders rips Clinton over Goldman Sachs ties," *The Hill*, January 17, 2016.

Feeling Their Pain. Jared McDonald, Oxford University Press. © Oxford University Press 2024.
DOI: 10.1093/oso/9780197696897.003.0005

to the voters. No doubt, voters can think of politicians who may have gone into public service for the right reasons (e.g., providing healthcare to those who need it, fighting for children suffering from abuse and neglect), but who upon obtaining power became more interested in keeping that power than enacting positive change. By casting Clinton's speeches to Wall Street firms in a suspicious light, political opponents could more credibly argue that Clinton's motives were no longer as altruistic as she claimed.

Casting further doubt on Clinton's genuine interest in the welfare of ordinary families was her unwillingness to disclose the content of those speeches. Sanders called on Clinton to release the transcripts, saying he would be happy to follow suit and release the transcripts for all his speeches to Wall Street firms (of which there were none).[4] This episode, while specific to the 2016 Democratic Primary, is not unique. Republicans in 2016 and 2012 also saw questions about transparency. These concerns were related to Donald Trump's and Mitt Romney's tax returns as well as their ties to foreign businesses. Both Republicans spent time on the campaign trail explaining why the lack of transparency was necessary or, at least, not as problematic as their opponents made them seem. The Clinton Foundation's ties to foreign governments were also questioned in 2016. Right or wrong, campaigns and other political organizations repeatedly exhibit a willingness to cast aspersions on their opponents' loyalties and desire for secrecy.

In this chapter, I seek to explain how Americans react to attacks that undermine perceptions of compassion. The theory I put forth here recognizes that, although candidates seek to portray themselves as caring, relatable individuals running for office to fix the problems everyday Americans face, those messages compete for attention with often contradictory messages from opposing candidates and other political adversaries. Furthermore, these messages are filtered through a news media that prefers to report on conflict and controversy over the types of positive messages the candidates might like to see reported (Cook 1998; Gans 1979).

In examining the effect of character attacks on public approval, I find that there are effective ways for candidates to rebut criticism, giving them a Teflon quality. In an era in which partisanship sometimes exerts an immense influence on voter behavior, politicians may be able to buttress any loss of public support among co-partisans by simply reminding them that elections are comparative exercises and the opposing side is worse.

---

[4] CNN Democratic Debate, April 14, 2016.

The implication here is that campaigns may be well served to fight fire with fire. Approval ratings often reflect support for one candidate compared to other politicians. Rather than try to rebut the claim that their candidate is "out of touch" with the average citizen, simply reminding co-partisans and independent citizens that they are better than the alternative may be an effective method for winning over voters. This creates something of a race-to-the-bottom effect: the moment a campaign launches a character attack, there is an incentive to strike back in equal measure, making the campaign less about the issues and more about a candidate's character and integrity in an electoral contest.

5.1 The Effect of Character Attacks

In Chapter 2, I showed that evaluations of candidate character clearly play a role in determining voter choice. In Chapter 3, I showed that perceptions of candidate character are malleable. Candidates have some agency over how they are perceived in the electorate and can leverage messages related to personal experience, emotion, and identity to convey either a universal sense of compassion or a compassion targeted at particular groups. Yet unexplored is the question of whether and how negative stories impact perceptions of a candidate's character. To date, there is mixed evidence whether the character attacks that often occur over the course of a campaign have any effect.

Research from Ansolabehere and Iyengar's (1995) *Going Negative* has shaped much of the debate over the past few decades regarding the effect of attack ads on voter choice and external efficacy. The findings presented there, namely that these sorts of attacks do little to influence voter choice but can undermine support for the electoral process, have been replicated across a range of electoral contexts (Abbe et al. 2000; Brader and Corrigan 2006; Chang 2003; Houston, Doan, and Roskos-Ewoldsen 1999; Krupnikov 2011; Lawton and Freedman 2001). Other research has pointed out issues with the findings, notably the findings on turnout and trust in the electoral process (Arceneaux and Nickerson 2010; Bartels 2000a; Brader 2005; Geer 2006; Niven 2005, 2006; Thorson et al. 2000).[5] Importantly, for the purposes of the present research, a number of laboratory experiments have found that

---

[5] Ultimately, the question of whether character attacks impact voter turnout or external efficacy is beyond the scope of this book, as I focus primarily on the means with which a politician can insulate their favorability in the face of a character attack.

attacks *can* harm the favorability and electability of the target of the ad (e.g., Basil, Schooler, and Reeves 1991; Brader 2005; Bullock 1994; Chang, Park, and Shim 1998; Kaid 1997; King and McConnell 2003; Shen and Wu 2002).

Central to the argument advanced in this chapter, however, is that candidates have tools at their disposal to fight back against negative character attacks. This may explain why, in contrast to much of the experimental research, the vast majority of observational work and field experiments conclude that attacks have little to no consequence on eventual voter choice (e.g., Arceneaux and Nickerson 2010; Capella and Taylor 1992; Crigler, Just, and Belt 2002; Kahn and Kenney 2004; Lau and Pomper 2004; Lau and Redlawsk 2005).

Here, I argue that the effect of character attacks on favorability often found in laboratory settings is not spurious but caution that these negative attacks can be easily countered. The effects these studies frequently find can be minimized or erased altogether in a more complex information environment where multiple messages compete with one another for attention. Campaigns rarely sit back while their candidates are under attack from political opponents, and as I will show, forcing respondents to view a politician in the context of another alternative can minimize the effect of political attacks.

5.2 Importance of Compassion in Elections

To understand why character attacks are effective in reducing political support, we first have to revisit why particular traits are desirable in a leader. I have argued that voters want certain qualities in political candidates, especially a capacity for compassion. These qualities tell Americans what type of leader the candidate will be (e.g., Holian and Prysby 2015; Kinder 1986). Politicians make hundreds of campaign promises, so the credibility of the politician is of great importance. If a voter believes that a particular politician truly cares about people like them, she will be less skeptical that any promises made by the candidate are empty. Compassion is conveyed through empathy, which can be effectively communicated with a commonality that bonds a message recipient to the speaker.

Because perceptions of compassion are related to candidate favorability and eventual voter choice, any opponent has a clear incentive to damage these perceptions of a political opponent. Opposing campaigns will look for stories that cast aspersions on their opponents' capacity for compassion. Any information that suggests a politician is not truly compassionate about the people she claims to champion is likely to damage positive evaluations.

During our discussion about what makes some politicians appear more compassionate than others, campaign communications professional Jimmy Donofrio referred to these types of attacks as a critical component of building a candidate's image. As a veteran of the Democratic National Committee's opposition research arm, Donofrio had played a role in the creation of several ads intended to portray Republican leaders as out of touch with the common person. He framed a successful attack as one that conveyed that an opponent was not just wrong but also malicious:

> I think that a good villain is one that is easily recognizable by your target audience. [Villains] are doing something that very directly impacts voters. In the case of the failed Obamacare repeal-and-replace efforts of the last couple weeks, the villains were all these Republicans who were trying to take away benefits from people and leave them out in the cold as far as their healthcare was concerned. It was about not caring for you. I'm going to take something away from you that will leave you worse off. And it doesn't impact me at all, because you [the taxpayer] pay for my healthcare, but I don't want to pay for yours.

As Donofrio suggests, attacks are not just about character or empathy specifically. They are about policies and tangible issues that are at stake for citizens. But policies do not enact themselves—politicians with motives, both good and bad, do. These motives are inextricably tied to compassion. As he puts it: about not caring for you.

Political professionals and the experimental literature show that these types of attacks on politicians have a negative effect on public approval. Yet the targets of such criticism have ways to blunt the effect of such attacks. The observed effect of character attacks in a controlled setting may not accurately capture the interplay that occurs when negative information is out there regarding most candidates for public office. Absolute levels of approval do not matter as much as the difference between the candidates in an election, and measurements of approval for a candidate may be influenced by comparisons to alternatives. Take, for example, evaluations of President Obama in his second term as president. In January 2016, before the Republican nominating process began in earnest, President Obama's approval rating hovered under 44%, with roughly 52% of the American public disapproving of his record (see Figure 5.1).

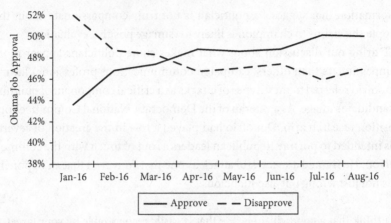

Figure 5.1 Obama Job Approval During Republican Nominating Process
Note: Numbers from the RealClearPolitics.com polling average.

While the campaign for the presidency started prior to this, beginning in January 2016 the media attention paid toward the campaigns grew dramatically as the first states held their primaries.[6] As the Democratic and GOP candidates went back and forth in their debates and the front-running Trump campaign found itself involved in media flaps over white supremacy and misogyny,[7] President Obama's approval numbers began to improve. While not directly tested in this book, many political pundits and Obama himself noted this rise in job approval,[8] attributing it largely to the fact that Americans were learning what the Republicans had to offer as an alternative. As Daniel Gross of *Fortune* put it, "rather than compare Obama to an idealized president, voters are increasingly evaluating his performance while contemplating the prospect of a President Donald Trump or President Hillary Clinton."[9]

In considering the effect of any political attack on a politician, I argue that it may be blunted by making voters think about the alternative in a similarly negative light. An attack on any politician's trustworthiness, integrity, and compassion may not be as persuasive as prior literature has suggested if it can be coupled with the suggestion that the alternative is no better. Put formally, I hypothesize the following:

---

[6] 2016 Campaign Television Tracker, created by Internet Archive's Television News Archive.
[7] "A working timeline of Donald Trump's campaign for the GOP nomination," *The Washington Examiner,* May 7, 2016.
[8] President Barack Obama address to the White House Correspondents Dinner, April 30, 2016.
[9] Daniel Gross, "Americans are falling in love with Barack Obama, again," *Fortune,* March 22, 2016.

H7. Teflon Hypothesis: Individuals who view a character attack against a politician will reduce their support for that politician. If the attack is viewed in conjunction with a character attack against a political opponent, approval will remain unaffected.

This argument usefully adds to existing literature, as past work has looked either at the effect of an individual negative attack or the macro effects of negativity in campaigns. The experiment I outline tests whether the effect of a real character attack used in the 2016 election can be blunted when voters are forced to consider the target of the attack in the context of a disliked alternative.

5.3 Research Design

I test the Teflon hypothesis using a survey experiment embedded in the 2016 Washington Post-University of Maryland (WP-UMD) poll aimed to be representative of the State of Maryland. The WP-UMD poll used probability sampling methodologies, combining 500 respondents from landline random-digit dialing, 500 respondents from cell phone random-digit dialing, and another 500 respondents pulled from the voter registration rolls. This ultimately yielded a total sample of 1,500 respondents, who were randomly assigned to one of three conditions: a control, a "Clinton criticism" condition, and a "Clinton + Trump criticism" condition.[10]

I designed this experiment to be as true to life as possible, using a real candidate for the presidency (Hillary Clinton) facing a criticism that was repeated often throughout the campaign: her connections to big banks were suspicious and the speeches she gave to Wall Street firms should be disclosed. By using a line of attack repeated often throughout the primary campaign, many respondents were likely familiar with the content of the treatment. As a consequence, the results should underestimate the true impact of this criticism if it were instead a completely new line of attack on Clinton. The control group received no information about Clinton's speeches to Wall Street firms, making responses to Clinton's capacity for compassion and favorability in this group an appropriate baseline for comparison.

---

[10] Due to the desire for journalistic integrity, some respondents received only the Trump criticism. These respondents were omitted from subsequent analyses, yielding an ultimate sample of 1,107. Results including the Trump criticism condition are included in the appendix to this chapter.

In the Clinton criticism condition, respondents answered a question regarding Clinton's paid speeches to big banks. To avoid bringing any evaluation of Donald Trump into the evaluation of Clinton, the criticism came from Clinton's primary opponent, Bernie Sanders:

> Bernie Sanders has said ordinary Americans are hurt by the political power of Wall Street and big banks. He criticized Hillary Clinton for giving $200,000 paid speeches to Wall Street firms and Clinton's refusal to provide transcripts of those speeches. Do you think Hillary Clinton should or should not disclose what she said in her speeches to Wall Street firms?

Responses to this question were ultimately unimportant to this experiment. Instead, this question served to prime respondents to think about Clinton's ties to big banks and wonder why she would choose not to disclose the content of those speeches to the public.

In the Clinton + Trump criticism condition, respondents were treated with the same question as before, but a new question was introduced to get individuals to consider Trump's trustworthiness and capacity for compassion as well.[11] In an attempt to make the two treatments as similar as possible, the criticism of Trump once again came from within the same party, using Mitt Romney's critique of Donald Trump's desire for secrecy:

> Former Republican presidential nominee Mitt Romney has called Donald Trump a fraud who would be bad for American workers, and said that Trump's refusal to release his tax returns is a sign he has something to hide. Do you think Donald Trump should or should not release his tax returns?

This treatment, importantly, says nothing about Hillary Clinton. Yet it should force respondents to consider Clinton's alternative when evaluating her candidacy and her ability to relate to others. Respondents rated Clinton on her ability to "care about people" like them. They were also asked whether they viewed her favorably or unfavorably overall. Responses were recoded from 0 to 1 for purposes of analysis.

---

[11] The survey treated respondents with the Clinton and Trump questions in random order.

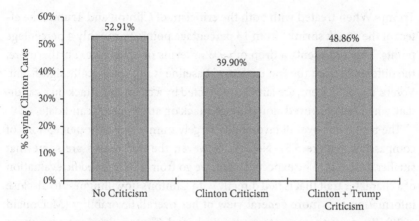

Figure 5.2 Perceptions of Clinton's Compassion by Condition

Note: Differences between the "Clinton Criticism" treatment and the "No Criticism" condition are statistically significant at $p<0.01$. Differences between the "Clinton + Trump Criticism" treatment and the "No Criticism" condition, however, are not statistically significant at conventional levels.

5.4 Teflon Hypothesis and Hillary Clinton

I first look to support for the Teflon hypotheses by comparing evaluations of Clinton's capacity for compassion across conditions. This evaluation is where we should find the greatest movement in perceptions of Clinton, as her speeches to Wall Street banks and her unwillingness to disclose the contents should speak directly to whether she truly cares about the average American rather than the wealthy elite (Figure 5.2).

In the control condition, where no criticism is leveled at Clinton, voter perceptions of her capacity for compassion are high. This is unsurprising given Maryland's left-leaning electorate, which Clinton ultimately won in the primary with over 62% of the Democratic vote. Among Maryland residents, nearly 53% of respondents believe that Clinton does, in fact, care about people like them. Yet when respondents are forced to think about Clinton's speeches to Wall Street banks and her unwillingness to provide transcripts of those speeches, less than 40% of respondents believe she cares about people like them. This 13-percentage-point effect is large when we remember that this attack had been widely circulated in the news, meaning many people in the control condition were at least somewhat aware of it.

Yet the Teflon hypothesis focuses on how campaigns can inoculate themselves from such criticism. This requires that the criticism of Clinton be accompanied with a criticism of her general election opponent, Donald

Trump. When treated with both the criticism of Clinton and Trump, the effect of the attack shrinks from 13 percentage points to roughly 4 percentage points. This represents a drop of 69% in terms of effect size. Furthermore, the difference from the "no criticism" baseline is not statistically significant. Voters, it would seem, are largely unaffected by a character attack on a candidate when it is conveyed alongside an attack on an opposing candidate.

The results for overall favorability largely mimic those for perceptions of compassion (Figure 5.3). Notably, however, the differences are somewhat smaller, which is to be expected when we go from a more specific evaluation of a character trait that is tied directly with Clinton's unwillingness to disclose information to a more general view of her overall favorability (McDonald 2020). There are some voters who likely feel Clinton does not care about people like them but still choose to find her generally more favorable because they like her for other reasons (experience, specific policy proposals, etc.). Clinton's favorability rating drops by just over 8 percentage points when she is criticized for speaking to Wall Street. This furthermore suggests that this line of attack from Bernie Sanders was effective in dampening support for the eventual nominee. Even when looking at something as general as overall favorability, these findings are consistent with experimental work demonstrating that character attacks are effective.

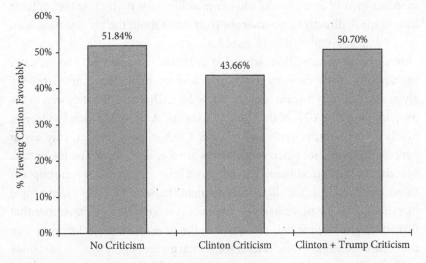

Figure 5.3 Clinton Favorability Rating by Condition

Note: Differences between the "Clinton Criticism" treatment and the "No Criticism" condition are statistically significant at $p<0.05$. Differences between the "Clinton + Trump Criticism" treatment and the "No Criticism" condition, however, are not statistically significant at conventional levels.

When we introduce Mitt Romney's criticism of Trump, however, this negative effect on Clinton goes away almost entirely. The difference between the control condition and the condition involving both critiques is barely more than 1 percentage point and statistically indistinguishable from zero. This finding, coupled with the results in the context of evaluations of a candidate's compassion, provide even stronger evidence of the Teflon hypothesis. When individuals who might be predisposed to support Clinton are forced to consider a character attack on her in the context of Donald Trump, the effect of that attack is blunted.

5.5 Teflon and the Perceptual Screen of Partisanship

The results thus far suggest that candidates may be able to effectively rebut any character attacks leveraged against them by making salient the character flaws in a political opponent. Despite this, looking at results in the aggregate can mask important movement among critical portions of the electorate. For this reason, I look at the effects of the two treatment conditions compared to the control by levels of partisanship.[12]

Treatment effects on Clinton's overall favorability are shown in Figure 5.4. The results for Democrats largely mirror the results for the full sample. The greater than 13-percentage-point negative effect for the Clinton criticism among Democrats is substantively large and statistically significant, yet it largely disappears among Democrats when the Trump criticism is introduced.

Given that elections are sometimes decided by a relatively small number of voters who occupy the middle of the political spectrum, the effects we see among independents are also of importance for Clinton's overall chances in any election. The results among these "pure independents" (people who claim not to lean toward either party) suggest that the trend that exists in the overall electorate is even more exaggerated among individuals in this key group.

The nearly 25-percentage-point negative effect is both substantively large and statistically significant. To put this in perspective, 45% of independents in the control group viewed Clinton favorably, which is a respectable but by

---

[12] In keeping with my theoretical expectations, as well as prior work on independent voters (Keith et al. 1992), I group "independent leaners" with partisans for this analysis.

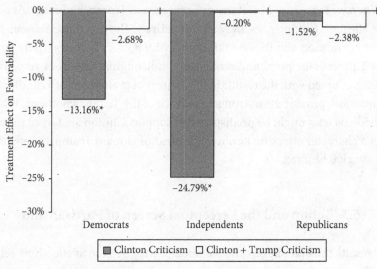

Figure 5.4 Effect of Clinton Criticism on Overall Favorability
*Effects are statistically significant at $p<0.05$.

no means great number for a politician as well-known as Clinton. Yet when provided information about Clinton's desire to keep the content of her Wall Street speeches a secret, those favorability ratings plummet to roughly 20%. This is only modestly better than the favorability ratings Republicans give Clinton (roughly 12.3%).

Despite the large degree to which this attack hurts Clinton's favorability among pure independents, the effect of the attack is entirely erased when independents consider it in the context of Donald Trump. This result makes sense when we consider what we know about independent voters, namely that they pay less attention to political news and are generally less engaged (Campbell et al. 1960; Keith et al. 1992), especially when it comes to a primary. When treated with negative information about Hillary Clinton, they react strongly. Yet when they are informed that the alternative may be just as bad, they modulate their views accordingly.

Finally, there is very little movement among Republicans for either of the conditions. Republicans have their minds made up about Clinton. As I noted, Republicans in the control only view Clinton favorably about 12% of the time. With that in mind, there simply is not much room for this group to move more negatively against her. Even though both of the treatment groups only viewed Clinton as favorable 10% of the time, the difference from this extremely low baseline was not statistically significant.

Ultimately, when we break out the aggregate results by levels of partisanship, we find trends that reinforce the initial results. Those who are most important to the Clinton electoral coalition (Democrats and independents) are the most likely to react negatively to an attack against her. Yet these groups are also the ones who come back to her once the character attack is coupled with negative information about her likely general election opponent, incentivizing the Clinton campaign and its allies to fight criticism with more criticism.

The implication of these results is that perceptions of compassion, as well as overall favorability, may be generated with competing factors in mind. In Chapter 3, I showed that politicians appear more compassionate when they convey a commonality that links them to citizens. What the results presented in this chapter suggest is that a politician can appear more compassionate simply by virtue of being compared to another candidate who is viewed as especially deficient in this character trait.

5.6 Summary

In this chapter, I have shown that perceptions of compassion are relative. Individuals do not exclusively evaluate candidates on an individual basis; instead, they consider the compassion of a politician in comparison to their opponent. As a result, when Hillary Clinton was criticized for her lack of empathy or ability to relate to the average voter, that message only damaged her insofar as it was received absent similar attacks against her political opponents.

I stop short, however, of arguing that it would always be in a campaign's self-interest to respond to a character attack with a character attack against an opponent. As prior research has found, attacks can backfire on the messenger (Basil, Schooler, and Reeves 1991; Chang, Park, and Shim 1998; Haddock and Zanna 1997; Houston, Doan, and Roskos-Ewoldsen 1999; Jasperson and Fan 2002; Shen and Wu 2002), especially if a candidate is seen as excessively negative (King and McConnell 2003). The attacks employed in the experiment did not include Hillary Clinton directly criticizing Donald Trump, nor do I have a direct measure of Bernie Sanders's approval before and after his criticism of Hillary Clinton. These results, when coupled with prior research in the field of political advertising, suggest that the most effective way to rebut character attacks is to have a third party criticize a political opponent. While this strategy may not always be available, the preponderance of the evidence suggests this will achieve the most favorable outcome for the preferred candidate.

Taken together with the evidence in earlier chapters, the data paint a nuanced picture for how perceptions of compassion are molded and remolded in a complex information environment. Campaigns convey messages about the personal histories of the candidates that appeal across the political spectrum. Yet, at the same time, opposition researchers for political opponents may find information that damages the empathetic stories around which campaigns seek to message. Attacks that undermine perceptions of compassion are most effective when they come absent any information that might undermine the reputation of a political opponent. That is, if a Republican running for a state legislative seat is accused of being in the pocket of special interests, voters may care far less if that information is accompanied by evidence that the Democratic opponent is similarly cozy with special interest groups. These attacks can sever the perception of commonality or, at the very least, make citizens view those commonalities as less relevant to the candidate's overall worldview. Undoubtedly, accusations of corruption do more than simply paint a politician as unempathetic—they may also shift perceptions of policy positions and the special interests she represents. But the results shown here demonstrate that these attacks cast doubt on whether a politician is doing her job because she cares about everyday people.

This incentive structure, where it is advantageous to respond to mudslinging with more mudslinging, is problematic if these types of attacks undermine faith in democratic institutions as prior research suggests (e.g., Krupnikov 2011). Yet some factors may mitigate the negative consequences of these types of attacks. First, the present research employed in-party criticism, which voters may deem especially credible but is less common in political discourse. Other sorts of attacks using either fabricated or exaggerated stories and developed by out-party groups should be less effective and therefore present less of an incentive for campaigns to mudsling. Additionally, I have not explored the features about the target of an attack that enhance or diminish the attack's effect. It may be that candidates who effectively convey compassion and who provide more transparency (disclose the content of paid speeches, tax returns, etc.) are less susceptible to these sorts of attacks, providing confidence that truly compassionate candidates can overcome highly negative campaigns.

Appendix: Survey Instrument and Results

2016 Washington Post-University of Maryland Survey

NOTE: The experiment involved four conditions. The first condition (the control) received neither the Clinton attack question nor the Trump attack question. The second condition received only the Clinton attack question. The third condition received only the Trump attack question. The fourth received the Clinton + Trump attack questions.

Treatment Wording

Clinton attack: Bernie Sanders has said ordinary Americans are hurt by the political power of Wall Street and big banks. He criticized Hillary Clinton for giving $200,000 paid speeches to Wall Street firms and Clinton's refusal to provide transcripts of those speeches. Do you think Hillary Clinton should or should not disclose what she said in her speeches to Wall Street firms?

1 Yes, should
2 No, should not
8 DK/No Opinion
9 NA/Refused

Trump attack: Former Republican presidential nominee Mitt Romney has called Donald Trump a fraud who would be bad for American workers, and said that Trump's refusal to release his tax returns is a sign he has something to hide. Do you think Donald Trump should or should not release his tax returns?

1 Yes, should
2 No, should not
8 DK/No Opinion
9 NA/Refused

Post-Treatment Question Wording

NOTE: For purposes of analysis, the following 4-point scales were recoded to be binary (favorable vs. unfavorable, well vs. not well). Results did not change substantially if full scale was used.

Overall, do you have a favorable or unfavorable impression of Hillary Clinton?

GET ANSWER AND ASK: Do you feel that way STRONGLY, or SOMEWHAT?

1 Strongly Favorable
2 Somewhat Favorable
3 Somewhat Unfavorable
4 Strongly Unfavorable
8 DK/No Opinion
9 NA/Refused

In your opinion, how well does the phrase, "she really cares about people like you" describe Hillary Clinton? (not well at all), (not too well), (pretty well), or (extremely well)?

1 Not well at all
2 Not too well
3 Pretty well
4 Extremely Well
8 DK/No Opinion
9 NA/Refused

Overall, do you have a favorable or unfavorable impression of Donald Trump?

GET ANSWER AND ASK: Do you feel that way STRONGLY, or SOMEWHAT?

1 Strongly Unfavorable
2 Somewhat Unfavorable
3 Somewhat Favorable
4 Strongly Favorable
8 DK/No Opinion
9 NA/Refused

In your opinion, how well does the phrase, "he really cares about people like you" describe Donald Trump? (not well at all), (not too well), (pretty well), or (extremely well)?

1 Not well at all
2 Not too well
3 Pretty well
4 Extremely Well
8 DK/No Opinion
9 NA/Refused

Results

Table A5.1 Mean Values of Dependent Variables of Interest by Condition

Condition	Clinton Cares	Clinton Favorability
No Criticism (Control)	0.529	0.518
(N=381)	(0.032)	(0.033)
Clinton Criticism	0.399	0.437
(N=355)	(0.033)	(0.034)
Trump Criticism	0.492	0.554
(N=396)	(0.032)	(0.032)
Clinton + Trump Criticism (N=371)	0.489	0.507
	(0.034)	(0.033)
N (Total)	1,471	1,459

Table A5.2 Randomization Check—Multinomial Logit Predicting
Assignment to Condition (Trump Criticism as Omitted Category,
Standard Errors in Parentheses)

Independent Variable	Control	Clinton Criticism	Clinton + Trump Criticism
Age	−0.002	0.003	−0.007
	(0.006)	(0.006)	(0.006)
Gender (Male)	−0.086	0.240	−0.158
	(0.208)	(0.204)	(0.215)
Education	0.167	0.134	0.079
	(0.106)	(0.111)	(0.107)
Race (white)	0.038	0.170	−0.071
	(0.372)	(0.376)	(0.360)
Race (Black)	0.129	0.035	−0.068
	(0.405)	(0.403)	(0.391)
Partisanship	0.148	0.170	0.024
	(0.126)	(0.125)	(0.129)
Income	−0.046	−0.033	−0.017
	(0.070)	(0.073)	(0.073)
Constant	−0.448	−1.029+	0.246
	(0.605)	(0.532)	(0.557)
Chi-Square	0.689		
N	1,176		

6

Compassion and Its Value for Politics

*Actor Mark Ruffalo: Let's say I'm walking along and, OH, I stubbed my
toe. Ohh that hurts!*

    *Murray Monster: Oh you poor thing. That hurts. I can imagine
exactly how you feel.*

    Ruffalo: That's it!

    Murray Monster: That's what?

    Ruffalo: That's empathy!

—Sesame Street[1]

Empathy in American society acts as a powerful social norm. Group empathy is found to drive acts of charity across social contexts (Nook et al.
2016) and support for redistributive economic policies that benefit less privileged individuals (Zhao, Ferguson, and Smillie 2017). When Michelle
Obama extolled the virtues of empathy at the 2020 Democratic National
Convention, she noted that our political leaders were supposed to live up to
the basic values we teach our children. This claim has merit. As the *Sesame
Street* epigraph demonstrates, empathy is one of the virtues we emphasize to
young children. Through early childhood socialization, we are taught that it
is important to understand the feelings of others and demand a degree of empathy from them as well. In adulthood, personal relationships with friends
and family are often defined by the degree to which we are able to show empathy for those who are experiencing some form of hardship.

This, I have shown, extends to our politics. We not only understand that
we are supposed to show empathy toward others in our community, but we
also expect others, particularly those entrusted to serve the community, to
show that same kind of empathy for those they represent. We expect and demand that politicians show some degree of understanding and caring, at least
toward those *we* care about, before we agree to vote for them.

In this book, I have sought to (1) provide a theory for why compassion
matters to voters, one that centers on questions of trust and low-information
rationality; (2) develop an understanding of why voters perceive some

---

[1] "Sesame Street: Mark Ruffalo: Empathy," YouTube, October 14, 2011.

Feeling Their Pain. Jared McDonald, Oxford University Press. © Oxford University Press 2024.
DOI: 10.1093/oso/9780197696897.003.0006

politicians as compassionate while others are viewed as aloof or unfeeling; (3) demonstrate that compassion matters in public approval and electoral accountability; and (4) assess the degree to which gender and campaign dynamics interact with messages about personal character to influence a candidate's public image.

When empathy leaves the friendly confines of *Sesame Street* and enters the realm of American politics, it takes on a self-interested quality. Voters are interested not only in whether a politician cares about others more generally but also whether the politician cares about people like them specifically. In this way, perceptions of empathy act as a heuristic, similar to how party cues or elite endorsements might. In some cases, the consequences are normatively desirable—we expect politicians to show empathy for those who are struggling and an understanding not only for what they need but also for how they feel. In other cases, the consequences are less positive: we understand that politics are often about how we distribute resources, and we are not only concerned with making sure we get our own "fair share," but that the people who are most like us also get what they deserve (and perhaps even more).

In developing this theory, I have portrayed voters as selfish actors: Americans want to know that a leader will be looking out for *their* interests and the interests of those they care about. In the case of economic appeals, such as understanding the concerns of saving for retirement, affording healthcare, or paying for a child's education, these concerns are nearly universal. Conveying empathy, or a personal connection, rather than sympathy is key to convincing a skeptical electorate that a politician truly cares.

Yet empathy is not always perceived through universal or near-universal appeals. When voters assess whether a candidate truly cares about people *like them,* they may be examining the degree to which they believe the politician will prioritize their interests over the interests of others. This means that a candidate need not express some universal love for all humanity. Instead, they can show preference for those individuals they need to win a majority of the vote. The presence of a commonality suggests that the politician is on their side and will consider their needs and the needs of those in their community. This leads citizens to view that politician as truly caring about people like them. The sources of commonality are varied but can be widely categorized as centering on experience, emotion, and identity.

It is worth discussing some important features of the American political system in light of these findings. How do perceptions of compassion fit in the broader scheme of democratic governance and electoral accountability? And how should we view the role of compassion in democratic governance given the ways it interacts with gender and partisanship to produce unexpected and sometimes undesirable outcomes?

6.1 The Importance of Empathy in the Context of Political Sophistication

The findings presented here are noteworthy in the context of political knowledge and electoral accountability. Scholars have long argued that Americans largely fail to live up to the ideals of civic citizenship. The modal American voter does not approach politics ideologically (Campbell et al. 1960; Converse [1964] 2006; Kinder and Kalmoe 2016). Beyond lacking opinions on many issues, Americans are often found to be unaware of basic political facts (Anson 2018; Delli Carpini, and Keeter 1996). Making matters worse, people do not seek out opposing views that might help them to become more informed, instead favoring poor information environments that reinforce their prior attitudes (Kuklinski et al. 2001; Mutz 2006).

It has been argued that these factors make voters ill-equipped to assign blame or give credit where it is due. Healy and Malhotra (2009), for example, find that voters reward politicians for responding to crises rather than preventing them, which creates inefficient policy outcomes. Although a negativity bias exists whereby people may focus more on a politician's failures than achievements (Weaver 1986), politicians may have methods at their disposal to avoid blame in situations where the news cycle has turned sour. For example, politicians may use subordinates as "lightning rods" (Ellis 1994) who can serve as the focal point of controversies and shield politicians from negative evaluations (see also Croco, McDonald, and Turitto 2022; Maestas et al. 2008). Worse, some have found that the highly partisan environment creates a situation where misinformation is not only easy to spread but that it also resonates among large swaths of the electorate (Berinsky 2017; Lenz 2012; Nyhan and Reifler 2010). Politicians who spread misinformation rarely pay a price for engaging in this practice (Croco, McDonald, and Turitto 2021; Nyhan et al. 2020; Wood and Porter 2018).

I have argued against this somewhat more pessimistic view of American democracy, arguing that some of the "randomness" of election outcomes Achen and Bartels (2016) point to can often hinge on perceptions of compassion. While some may consider evaluations of candidate character to be a normatively undesirable criteria upon which to select a leader or legislator, I have shown that these perceptions are not random but respond predictably to political stimuli. Voters are able to infer the degree to which a candidate is empathetic, and by extension compassionate, by the characteristics of that politician, both those visible and some less visible. I find that empathetic appeals, driven by some sort of commonality, lead to significantly higher evaluations of candidate compassion. These empathetic appeals may be manipulated by skilled politicians and campaigns, though campaign history shows that the ability to manipulate the voting public into believing a candidate is empathetic comes with risk. Many politicians have had empathetic appeals backfire when they are seen as inauthentic or insincere.

These perceptions are not random, and, I argue here that they are not as normatively problematic as a heuristic for voters to use as some may believe. It is, after all, unrealistic to expect that voters will develop constrained ideologies or strong opinions on a sufficient number of policies to arrive at a "correct" voting decision. Holian and Prysby (2015) go a step further, arguing that voters who use opinions on public policy to guide their votes may actually arrive at worse voting decisions than those who rely on assessments of candidate character. They use the example of the 2000 election to make this point. In 2000, surveys showed that voters were basing their choice largely on economic considerations. Yet voters could not have foreseen the impact that 9/11 would have on politics. In retrospect, opinions about foreign policy and national security should have been more salient for voting decisions in 2000, but voters could not predict the future. Less sophisticated voters, who may have cast their vote not based on a preferred economic policy but based on their assessments of candidate character, however, would likely not have regretted their vote choice. Regardless of what issue is most salient, political character should remain relatively constant.

6.2 What Compassion Means for Electoral Competition amid Partisan Polarization

While most Americans are not highly informed or ideologically constrained in their political thinking, most scholars working in the field of American political behavior agree that polarization is not exclusively a phenomenon among political elites. Americans themselves are deeply and evenly divided between their two camps, such that out-group antipathy and in-group pref-erence can grow even if true policy disagreement is absent (Mason 2018; Iyengar, Sood, and Lelkes 2012). Barack Obama's assertion in 2012 that "we are not as divided as our politics suggest,"[2] while aspirational, is not supported by the evidence. Whether he was unaware of the nature of our polarized politics or simply unwilling to express this more pessimistic point of view publicly, the American public truly is deeply entrenched in par-tisan camps.

Empathy, I posit, provides some hope for bridging a deep partisan divide. While empathy is not a panacea for political polarization, it represents a meaningful step forward toward more civil discourse and more functional government. Perceptions of compassion, driven by empathy, are highly in-fluential in determining voting decisions among independent voters who often represent the swing voting bloc in any election. Empathetic appeals, furthermore, do not need to be divisive. With experiential empathy, for ex-ample, I show how broad economic appeals to help all struggling Americans resonate with citizens, and they most especially resonate when the politician belongs to the opposing party of the voter.

In the past, the commonsense approach to appealing to "moderates" was to take a moderate issue stance. In the era of well-sorted party coalitions, taking moderate stances can hurt politicians among activists within their party. Furthermore, there is little evidence that independent voters, who are on average less politically knowledgeable than partisans, will be swayed by token attempts to moderate an issue stance. Recent research suggests that even those who claim to be "moderate" are not truly moderate but are instead cross-pressured (Broockman 2016). They often hold extreme views, but those views do not align consistently with one party or the other. As a result, moderating one's policy stances is unlikely to appeal to this group of voters.

Instead, politicians may see the greatest electoral payoff by appealing to the humanity of those predisposed to be skeptical of their candidacy. When politicians show that they share the values and experiences of those who are most predisposed to dislike them *and* receive a payoff in terms of the public image, it incentivizes political elites to raise the bar of discourse in this country and hopefully decreases the degree of vitriol we see in our politics, both at the elite level and among the masses.

---

[2] Barack Obama victory speech, November 6, 2012.

6.3 What Compassion Means for Women Seeking Elected Office

The findings in Chapter 4 suggest that women are at a decided disadvantage when it comes to portraying their personal characteristics publicly. Although they may be perceived as more compassionate, this stereotype ultimately harms their ability to message around other traits that are perceived to be masculine. Men do not face such constraints. They are rewarded for emphasizing all positive character traits regardless of whether they are traditionally perceived as masculine or feminine.

This finding fits in a long line of research that shows the unique barriers women face in politics. Female incumbents face more challenges and more qualified challengers than their male counterparts (Milyo and Schosberg 2000; Palmer and Simon 2010) but are just as likely to win (e.g., Carroll, 1994). Women tend to be more qualified than men in Congress (Bauer 2020; Conroy 2015; Holman, Merolla, and Zechmeister 2011; 2016). Despite gender bias, gender stereotypes, and negative public perceptions of women handling stereotypical "masculine" issues (e.g., Huddy and Terkildsen 1993), Atkinson and Windett (2019) find female members of Congress propose more bills and have broader policy agendas than men. Penalizing women for going against type means that important voices, who not only represent critical portions of the citizenry but also bring greater qualifications, more legislation, and a broader array of policy expertise could be lost in policy debates.

The source of gender bias is deeply embedded in society. These barriers and stereotypes can only be addressed through greater representation of women in leadership roles, such that these positions are not viewed through a gendered lens. Advocacy groups such as She Should Run—organizations that work to level the playing field for women seeking leadership positions—can play a critical role in this effort. And although I focus on perceptions of compassion of those holding elected office, new policies ensuring the representation of women on the boards of publicly owned entities may also help erode the perception of leadership as a masculine trait.[3]

Women continue to face gendered expectations and to be underrepresented in leadership in both elected and career public positions. However, women bring a unique leadership perspective. Women leaders tend to take a transformational approach (Eagly, Joannesen-Schmidt, and Van Engen 2003;

---

[3] For an example of this, see AB 979 in California.

Potter and Volden 2021) and be more inclusive leaders (Fox and Schuhmann 1999). Greater representation of women has been found to increase citizen coproduction (Riccucci, Van Ryzin, and Li 2016) and enhance citizen trust (Riccucci, Van Ryzin, and Lavena 2014). In the political realm, Lawless, Theriault, and Guthrie (2018) find greater collegiality among women despite little influence on bipartisanship. This may in part be due to today's extreme political polarization. As more women enter leadership positions and younger generations of American women become more engaged in politics (Deckman 2020), perhaps politics and management will become less masculine, or at least more supportive of women, so women can freely lead without adhering to or compensating for gender stereotypes.

6.4 Summary

Despite the power of partisanship to shape our attitudes toward candidates and determine political behavior, I have argued that the power of personal character is not diminished. If anything it has grown in importance as small shifts in individual attitudes can have major implications for aggregate outcomes.

If there are any lessons for democratic governance to be learned, it is that decisions made by citizens based on evaluations of compassion can be both biased and rational. Bias, whether it is pigeon-holing women as compassionate nurturers rather than strong leaders or refusing to believe that a Black politician could care about white working-class citizens even in the presence of experiential commonalities, provides the greatest cause for concern about a compassion-centric model of political behavior. These shortcomings may lead voters to make decisions that hurt them and create a barrier to inclusion in all levels of American government. The research here does not speak directly to approaches for reducing bias and stereotyping in the United States. Yet unless negative stereotypes are confronted, it is very likely that inefficient election outcomes will continue in the future.

Yet the basic assumption made by voters that compassionate politicians will bring about the greatest personal outcomes, in its most basic form, is a rational one. It may at times be faulty, but it is hard to argue that these assumptions are any faultier than those assumptions regarding policy preferences, retrospective assessments of performance, or prospective evaluations. And in a political environment where few citizens spend time directly getting to know the officials entrusted with the power of government, using commonalities to inform perceptions is similarly rational. The work ahead does not lie in convincing voters to use different strategies, but in offering voters clearer, unvarnished pictures of who the candidates are and with whom the candidates identify.

References

Aaldering, Loes, and Rens Vliegenthart. 2016. "Political Leaders and the Media. Can We Measure Political Leadership Images in Newspapers Using Computer-Assisted Content Analysis?" *Quality and Quantity* 50: 1871–1905.

Abbe, Owen, Paul Herrnson, David Magleby, and Kelly Patterson. 2000. "Campaign Professionalism, Negative Advertising, and Electoral Success in U.S. House Races." Presented at the annual meeting of the Midwest Political Science Association, April 27, 2020.

Abele, Andrea E. 2003. "The Dynamics of Masculine-Agentic and Feminine-Communal Traits: Findings from a Prospective Study." *Journal of Personality and Social Psychology* 85: 768–776.

Abele, Andrea E., Amy J.C. Cuddy, Charles M. Judd, and Vincent Yzerbyt. 2008. "Fundamental dimensions of social judgment." *European Journal of Social Psychology* 38: 1063–1065.

Abramowitz, Alan I. 2012. "Forecasting in a Polarized Era: The Time for Change Model and the 2012 Presidential Election." *PS: Political Science and Politics* 45(4): 618–619.

Abramowitz, Alan, David J. Lanoue, and Subha Ramesh. 1988. "Economic Conditions, Causal Attributions, and Political Evaluations in the 1984 Presidential Election." *Journal of Politics* 50: 848–863.

Achen, Chrisopher H., and Larry M. Bartels. 2016. *Democracy for Realists: Why Elections Do Not Produce Responsive Government*. Princeton: Princeton University Press.

Alexander, Deborah, and Kristi Andersen. 1993. "Gender as a Factor in the Attribution of Leadership Traits." *Political Research Quarterly* 46(3): 527–545.

Ansolabehere, Stephen, and Shanto Iyengar. 1995. *Going Negative: How Political Advertisements Shrink and Polarize the Electorate*. New York: Free Press.

Ansolabehere, Stephen, and Douglas Rivers. 2013. "Cooperative Survey Research." *Annual Review of Political Science* 16(2): 307–329.

Anson Ian G. 2018. "Partisanship, Political Knowledge, and the Dunning-Kruger Effect." *Political Psychology*. Online First.

Arceneaux, Kevin, and David W. Nickerson. 2010. "Comparing Negative and Positive Campaign Messages: Evidence from Two Field Experiments." *American Politics Research* 38(1): 54–83.

Atkinson, Mary Layton, and Jason Harold Windett. 2019. "Gender stereotypes and the policy priorities of women in congress." *Political Behavior* 41(3): 769–789.

Banks, Antoine. 2014. *Anger and Racial Politics: The Emotional Foundation of Racial Attitudes in America*. New York: Cambridge University Press.

Barnes, Tiffany D., Emily Beaulieu, and Gregory W. Saxton. 2020. "Sex and Corruption: How Sexism Shapes Voters' Responses to Scandal." *Politics, Groups, and Identities* 8(1): 103–121.

Barreto, Matt A., Gary M. Segura, and Nathan D. Woods. 2004. "The Mobilizing Effect of Majority-Minority Districts on Latino Turnout." *American Political Science Review* 98 (Feb.): 65–75.

Bartels, Larry M. 2000a. "Campaign Quality: Standards for Evaluation, Benchmarks for Reform." In *Campaign Reform: Insights and Evidence*, ed. Larry M. Bartels and Lynn Vavreck. Ann Arbor: University of Michigan Press, 1–61.

Bartels, Larry M. 2000b. "Partisanship and Voting Behavior." *American Journal of Political Science* 44(1): 35–50.

Bartels, Larry M. 2002. "Beyond the Running Tally: Partisan Bias in Political Perceptions." *Political Behavior* 24(2): 117–150.

Basil, Michael, Caroline Schooler, and Byron Reeves. 1991. "Positive and Negative Political Advertising: Effectiveness of Ads and Perceptions of Candidates." In *Television and Political Advertising*, Vol. 1, ed. Frank Biocca. Hillsdale, NJ: Lawrence Erlbaum, 245–262.

Batson, C. Daniel. 1991. *The Altruism Question: Toward a Social-Psychological Answer.* Hillsdale, NJ: Erlbaum.

Batson, C. Daniel, and Nadia Y. Ahmad. 2009. "Using Empathy to Improve Intergroup Attitudes and Relations." *Social Issues and Policy Review* 3(1): 141–177.

Batson, C. Daniel, Bruce D. Duncan, Paula Ackerman, Terese Buckley, and Kimberly Birch. 1981. "Is Empathetic Emotion a Source of Altruistic Motivation." *Journal of Personality and Social Psychology* 40(2): 290–302.

Batson, C. Daniel, Shannon Early, and Giovanni Salvarani. 1997. "Perspective Taking: Imagining How Another Feels Versus Imagining How You Would Feel." *Personality and Social Psychology Bulletin* 23(7): 751–758.

Batson, C. Daniel, Jim Fultz, and Patricia Schoenrade. 1987. "Distress and Empathy: Two Qualitatively Distinct Vicarious Emotions with Different Motivational Consequences." *Journal of Personality* 55(1): 19–39.

Bauer, Nichole M. 2020. "Shifting Standards: How Voters Evaluate the Qualifications of Female and Male Candidates." *Journal of Politics* 82(1): 1–12.

Best, Deborah L., and John E. Williams. 1990. *Measuring Sex Stereotypes: A Thirty-Nation Study.* Beverly Hills, CA: Sage.

Berelson, Bernard R., Paul F. Lazarsfeld, and William N. McPhee. 1954. *Voting: A Study of Opinion Formation in a Presidential Campaign.* Chicago: University of Chicago Press.

Berinsky, Adam J. 2017. "Rumors and Health Care Reform: Experiments in Political Misinformation." *British Journal of Political Science* 47(2): 241–262.

Berinsky, Adam, Gregory Huber, and Gabriel Lenz. 2012. "Evaluating Online Labor Markets for Experimental Research: Amazon.com's Mechanical Turk." *Political Analysis* 20: 351–368.

Bernhardt, Boric C., and Tania Singer. "The Neural Basis of Empathy." *Annual Review of Neuroscience* 35: 1–23.

Bishop, Bill, and Robert G. Cushing. 2009. *The Big Sort: Why the Clustering of Like-Minded America Is Tearing Us Apart.* Boston: Mariner Books.

Brader, Ted. 2005. "Striking a Responsive Chord: How Political Ads Motivate and Persuade Voters by Appealing to Emotions." *American Journal of Political Science* 49 (Apr.): 388–405.

Brader, Ted, and Bryce Corrigan. 2006. "How the Emotional Tenor of Ad Campaigns Affects Political Participation." Presented at the annual meeting of the American Political Science Association, August 31–September 3, 2006, Philadelphia.

Broockman, David E. "Approaches to Studying Policy Representation." *Legislative Studies Quarterly* 41(1): 181–215.

Brooks, Deborah Jordan. 2013. *He Runs, She Runs: Why Gender Stereotypes Do Not Harm Women Candidates*. Princeton: Princeton University Press.

Bullock, David A. 1994. "The Influence of Political Attack Advertising on Undecided Voters: An Experimental Study of Campaign Message Strategy." Unpublished PhD diss., University of Arizona.

Burgoon, Judee K. 1993. "Interpersonal Expectations, Expectancy Violations, and Emotional Communication." *Journal of Language and Social Psychology* 12(1): 30–48.

Burnham, Walter Dean. 1989. "The Reagan Heritage." In *The Election of 1988: Reports and Interpretations*, ed. Gerald M. Pomper et al. Chatham, NJ: Chatham House.

Byrne, Donn. 1971. *The Attraction Paradigm*. New York: Academic Press.

Campbell, Angus, Philip Converse, Warren Miller, and Donald Stokes. 1960. *The American Voter*. New York: Wiley.

Campbell, James E. 1983. "Candidate Image Evaluations: Influence and Rationalization in Presidential Primaries." *American Politics Quarterly* 11 (July): 293–313.

Campbell, James. 2012. "Forecasting the Presidential and Congressional Elections of 2012: The Trial-Heat and the Seats-in-Trouble Models." *PS: Political Science & Politics* 45(4): 630–634.

Capella, Louis, and Ronald D. Taylor. 1992. "An Analysis of the Effectiveness of Negative Political Campaigning." *Business and Public Affairs* 18 (Spring): 10–17.

Carroll, Susan J. 1994. *Women as candidates in American politics*. Bloomington: Indiana University Press.

Cassese, Erin C., and Mirya R. Holman. 2018. "Party and Gender Stereotypes in Campaign Attacks." *Political Behavior* 40(3): 785–807.

Chang, Chingching. 2003. "Party Bias in Political-Advertising Processing." *Journal of Advertising* 32(2): 55–67.

Chang, Won Ho, JaeJin Park, and SungWook Shim. 1998. "Effectiveness of Negative Political Advertising." Unpublished manuscript, Ohio University.

Clifford, Scott. 2018. "Reassessing the Structure of Presidential Character." *Electoral Studies* 54: 240–247.

Conroy, Meredith. 2015. *Masculinity, Media and the American Presidency*. New York: Palgrave MacMillan.

Converse, Philip E. (1964) 2006. "The Nature of Belief Systems in Mass Publics." *Critical Review* 18(1–3): 1–74.

Cook, Timothy E. 1998. *Governing with the News: The News Media as a Political Institution*. Chicago: University of Chicago Press.

Cooper, Robert K., and Ayman Sawaf. 1997. *Executive EQ: Emotional Intelligence in Leadership and Organizations*. New York: Grosset/Putman.

Cramer, Katherine J. 2016. *The Politics of Resentment: Rural Consciousness in Wisconsin and the Rise of Scott Walker*. Chicago: University of Chicago Press.

Croco, Sarah E., Michael J. Hanmer, and Jared McDonald. 2020. "At What Cost? Reexamining Audience Costs in Realistic Settings." *Journal of Politics*. Online.

Croco, Sarah E., Jared McDonald, and Candace Turitto. 2022. "The Face of the Problem: How Subordinates Shield Executives from Blame." *Journal of Experimental Political Science* 9(3): 359–368.

Croco, Sarah E., Jared McDonald, and Candace Turitto. 2021. "Making Them Pay: Using the Norm of Honesty to Generate Costs for Political Lies." *Electoral Studies* 69: 102250.

Crigler, Ann, Marion Just, and Todd Belt. 2002. "The Three Faces of Negative Campaigning: The Democratic Implications of Attack Ads, Cynical News, and Fear Arousing Messages." Presented at the annual meeting of the American Political Science Association, August 2–September 1, 2002, Boston.

Cuff, Benjamin M. P., Sarah J. Brown, Laura Taylor, and Douglas J. Howat. 2016. "Empathy: A Review of the Concept." *Emotion Review* 8: 144–153.

Dafoe, Allan, Baobao Zhang, and Devin Caughey. 2018. "Information Equivalence in Survey Experiments." *Political Analysis* 26(4): 399–416.

Davis, Mark H. 1983. "Measuring Individual Differences in Empathy: Evidence for a Multidimensional Approach." *Journal of Personality and Social Psychology* 44(1): 113–126.

Davis, Mark H. 2009. "Empathy." In *Encyclopedia of Human Relationships*, ed. Harry T. Reis and Susan Sprecher. Thousand Oaks, CA: Sage, 516–520.

Dawson, Michael C. 1994. *Behind the Mule: Race and Class in African-American Politics*. Princeton: Princeton University Press.

Deckman, Melissa. 2020. "IGNITE Survey of Generation Z Women and Men." IGNITE https://www.ignitenational.org/our_research.

Deckman, Melissa M., and Michele L. Swers. 2019. *Women and Politics: Paths to Power and Political Influence*. Lanham, MD: Rowman & Littlefield.

DeHart-Davis, Leisha, Deneen Hatmaker, Kimberly L. Nelson, Sanjay K. Pandey, Sheela Pandey, and Amy E. Smith. 2020. *Gender Imbalance in Public Sector Leadership*. Elements in Public and Nonprofit Administration. Cambridge: Cambridge University Press.

Delli Carpini, Michael X. and Scott Keeter. 1996. *What Americans Know About Politics and Why It Matters*. New Haven, CT: Yale University Press.

Dolan, Kathleen. 2004. *Voting for Women: How the Public Evaluates Women Candidates*. Boulder, CO: Westview Press.

Dolan Kathleen. 2014. "Gender Stereotypes, Candidate Evaluations and Voting for Women Candidates: What Really Matters?" *Political Research Quarterly* 67(1): 96–107.

Downs, Anthony. 1957. *An Economic Theory of Democracy*. New York: HarperCollins.

Eagly, Alice H. 1987. *Sex Differences in Social Behavior: A Social-Role Interpretation*. Hillsdale, NJ: Erlbaum.

Eagly, Alice H., Mary C. Johannesen-Schmidt, and Marloes L. Van Engen. 2003. "Transformational, Transactional, and Laissez-Faire Leadership Styles: A Meta-Analysis Comparing Women and Men." *Psychological Bulletin* 129(43): 569.

Eagly, Alice H., and Steven J. Karau. "Role Congruity Theory of Prejudice Toward Female Leaders." *Psychological Review* 109(3): 573–598.

Eisenberg, Nancy. 2000. "Emotion, Regulation, and Moral Development." *Annual Review of Political Psychology* 51: 665–697.

Ellis, Richard J. 1994. *Presidential Lightning Rods: The Politics of Blame Avoidance*. Lawrence: University of Kansas Press.

Erikson, Robert S., and Christopher Wlezien. 2012. "The Objective and Subjective Economy and the Presidential Vote." *PS: Political Science & Politics* 45(4):620–624.

Erikson, Robert S., Michael B. MacKuen, and James A. Stimson. 2002. *The Macro Polity*. New York: Cambridge University Press.

Fenno Jr., Richard F. 1978. *Home Style: House Members in Their Districts*. Boston: Little, Brown.

Ferejohn, John A. 1986. "Incumbent Performance and Electoral Control." *Public Choice* 50: 5–26.

Fiorina, Morris P., and Abrams, Samuel J. 2008. "Political Polarization in the American Public." *Annual Review of Political Science* 11:563–588.

Fox, Richard L., and Zoe Oxley. 2003. "Gender Stereotyping in State Executive Elections." *Journal of Politics* 65(3): 833–850.

Fox, Richard L., and Robert A. Schuhmann. 1999. "Gender and Local Government: A Comparison of Women and Men City Managers." *Public Administration Review* 59(3): 231–242.

Frable, Deborrah E. S. 1997. "Gender, Racial, Ethnic, Sexual, and Class Identities." *Annual Review of Psychology* 48: 139–162.

Funk, Carolyn L. 1996. "The Impact of Scandal on Candidate Evaluations: An Experimental Test of the Role of Candidate Traits." *Political Behavior* 18(1): 1–24.

Funk, Carolyn L. 1997. "Implications of Political Expertise in Candidate Trait Evaluations." *Political Research Quarterly* 50(3): 675–697.

Funk, Carolyn L. 1999. "Bringing the Candidate into Models of Candidate Evaluation." *Journal of Politics* 61(3): 700–720.

Gay, Claudine, Jennifer Hochschild, and Ariel White. 2016. "Americans' Belief in Linked Fate: Does the Measure Capture the Concept?" *Journal of Race, Ethnicity, and Politics* 1(1): 117–144.

Gabora Liane, Eleanor Rosch, and Diederik Aerts. 2008. "Toward an Ecological Theory of Concepts." *Ecological Psychology* 20(1): 84–116.

Gans, Herbert. 1979. *Deciding What's News: A Study of CBS Evening News, NBC Nightly News, Newsweek and Time.* New York: Vintage.

Geer, John G. 2006. *In Defense of Negativity: Attack Ads in Presidential Campaigns.* Chicago: University of Chicago Press.

George, Jennifer M. 2000. "Emotions and Leadership: The Role of Emotional Intelligence." *Human Relations* 53(8): 1027–1055.

Gilovich, Thomas, Dale Griffin, and Daniel Kahneman. 2002. *Heuristics and Biases: The Psychology of Intuitive Judgment.* Cambridge: Cambridge University Press.

Goleman, Daniel.1998. *Working with Emotional Intelligence.* New York: Bantam Books.

Gonzalez, Frank J. 2020. "Unresolved Politics: Implicit Ambivalence and Political Cognition." *Political Research Quarterly.* Online.

Goren, Paul. 2002. "Character Weakness, Partisan Bias, and Presidential Evaluation." *American Journal of Political Science* 46 (July): 627–641.

Goren, Paul. 2007. "Character Weakness, Partisan Bias, and Presidential Evaluation: Modifications and Extensions." *Political Behavior* 29 (Sept.): 305–326.

Graham, Jesse, Jonathan Haidt, and Brian A. Nosek. 2009. "Liberals and Conservatives Rely on Different Sets of Moral Foundations." *Journal of Personality and Social Psychology* 9(5): 1029–1046.

Green, Donald P., Bradley Palmquist, and Eric Schickler. 2002. *Partisan Hearts and Minds: Political Parties and the Social Identities of Voters.* New Haven, CT: Yale University Press.

Greene, Steven. 2001. "The Role of Character Assessments in Presidential Approval." *American Politics Research* 29(2): 196–210.

Guy, Mary Ellen. 1995. "Hillary, Health Care, and Gender Power." In *Gender Power, Leadership, and Governance,* ed. G. Duerst-Lahti and R. M. Kelly. Ann Arbor: University of Michigan Press, 239–256.

Haddock, Geoffrey, and Mark P. Zanna. 1997. "Impact of Negative Advertising on Evaluations of Political Candidates: The 1993 Canadian Federal Election." *Basic and Applied Social Psychology* 19(3): 204–223.

Haidt, Jonathan. 2012. *The Righteous Mind: Why Good People Are Divided by Politics and Religion.* New York: Knopf Doubleday Publishing Group.

Haidt, Jonathan, and Craig Joseph. 2004. "Intuitive Ethics: How Innately Prepared Intuitions Generate Culturally Variable Virtues." *Daedalus: Special Issue on Human Nature* 133(4): 55–66.

Halperin, Mark, and John Heilemann. 2013. *Double Down: Game Change 2012.* New York: Penguin.

Hanmer, Michael J., and Ozan K. Kalkan. 2013. "Behind the Curve: Clarifying the Best Approach to Calculating Predicted Probabilities and Marginal Effects from Limited Dependent Variable Models." *American Journal of Political Science* 57(1): 263–277.

Hayes, Danny. 2011 "When Gender and Party Collide: Stereotyping in Candidate Trait Attribution." *Politics & Gender* 7(2):133–165.

Hayes, Danny. 2005. "Candidate Qualities Through a Partisan Lens: A Theory of Trait Ownership." *American Journal of Political Science* 49 (Oct.): 908–923.

Healy, Andrew, and Neil Malhotra. 2009. "Myopic Voters and Natural Disaster Policy." *American Political Science Review* 103(3): 387–406.

Hein, Grit, and Tania Singer. 2008. "I Feel How You Feel but Not Always: The Empathic Brain and Its Modulation." *Current Opinion in Neurobiology* 18(2): 153–158.

Hetherington, Marc J. 2001. "Resurgent Mass Partisanship: The Role of Elite Polarization." *American Political Science Review* 95(3): 619–631.

Hibbing, John R., and John R. Alford. 1981. "The Electoral Impact of Economic Conditions: Who Is Held Responsible?" *American Journal of Political Science* 25(3): 423–439.

Hibbing, John R., and Elizabeth Theiss-Morse. 2002. *Stealth Democracy: Americans' Beliefs About How Government Should Work.* Cambridge: Cambridge University Press.

Holian, David B., and Charles Prysby. 2011. "Character First: Rethinking John McCain's 2008 Campaign Strategy." *American Review of Politics* 32 (Fall 2011/Winter 2012): 318–342.

Holian, David B., and Charles Prysby. 2014. "Candidate Character Traits in the 2012 Presidential Election." *Presidential Studies Quarterly* 44(3): 484–505.

Holian, David B., and Charles Prysby. 2015. *Candidate Character Traits in Presidential Elections.* New York: Routledge.

Holland, John L. 1959. "A Theory of Vocational Choice." *Journal of Counseling Psychology* 6(1): 35–45.

Holman, Mirya R., Jennifer Merolla, and Elizabeth Zechmeister. 2011."Sex, Stereotypes, and Security: An Experimental Study of the Effect of Crises on Assessments of Gender and Leadership." *Journal of Women, Politics, and Policy* 32(3):173–192.

Holman, Mirya R., Jennifer Merolla, and Elizabeth Zechmeister. 2017. "Can Experience Overcome Stereotypes in Times of Terror Threat?" *Research & Politics* 4(1): 1–7.

Hopkins, Daniel J., and Hans Noel. 2022. "Trump and the Shifting Meaning of 'Conservative': Using Activists' Pairwise Comparisons to Measure Politicians' Perceived Ideologies." *American Political Science Review*. Online.

Houston, David A., Kelly Doan, and David Roskos-Ewoldsen. 1999. "Negative Political Advertising and Choice Conflict." *Journal of Experimental Psychology: Applied* 5(1): 3–16.

Huddy, Leonie. 2001. "From Social to Political Identity: A Critical Examination of Social Identity Theory." *Political Psychology* 22: 127–156.

Huddy, Leonie, and Alexa Bankert. 2017. "Political Partisanship as a Social Identity." *Oxford Research Encyclopedia of Politics*. Online.

Huddy, Leonie, Lilliana Mason, and Lene Aaroe. 2015."Expressive Partisanship: Campaign Involvement, Political Emotion, and Partisan Identity." *American Political Science Review* 109: 1–17.

Huddy, Leonie, and Nayda Terkildsen. 1993. "Gender Stereotypes and the Perception of Male and Female Candidates." *American Journal of Political Science* 37(1): 119–147.

Hunt, Charles. 2021. "Expanding Constituency Support Through Shared Local Roots in U.S. House Primaries." *American Politics Research* 49(2): 233–244.

Iyengar, Shanto, and Masha Krupenkin. 2018. "The Strengthening of Partisan Affect." *Political Psychology* 39(S1): 201–218.

Iyengar, Shanto, Guarav Sood, and Yphtach Lelkes. 2012. "Affect, Not Ideology: A Social Identity Perspective on Polarization." *Public Opinion Quarterly* 76(3): 405–431.

Jackman, Simon, and Bradley Spahn. 2014. "Why Does the American National Election Study Overestimate Voter Turnout?" Political Methodology Meetings, University of Georgia.

Jamieson, Kathleen Hall. 1995. *Beyond the Double Bind: Women and Leadership*. Oxford: Oxford University Press.

Jardina, Ashley. 2019. *White Identity Politics*. New York: Cambridge University Press.

Jasperson, Amy E., and David P. Fan. 2002. "An Aggregate Examination of the Backlash Effect in Political Advertising: The Case of the 1996 U.S. Senate Race in Minnesota." *Journal of Advertising* 31(2): 1–12.

Jerit, Jennifer, Jason Barabas, and Toby Bolsen. 2006. "Citizens, Knowledge, and the Information Environment." *American Journal of Political Science* 50(2): 266–282.

Jones, Philip Edward. 2014. "Revisiting Stereotypes of Non-White Politicians' Ideological and Partisan Orientations." *American Politics Research* 42(2): 283–310.

Kahn, Kim, and Patrick J. Kenney. 2004. *No Holds Barred: Negativity in U.S. Senate Campaigns*. Upper Saddle River, NJ: Pearson Prentice Hall.

Kaid, Lynda Lee. 1997. "Effects of the Television Spots on Images of Dole and Clinton." *American Behavioral Scientist* 40(2): 1085–1094.

Karl, Kristyn L., and Timothy J. Ryan. 2016. "When Are Stereotypes About Black Candidates Applied? An Experimental Test." *Journal of Race, Ethnicity and Politics* 1(2): 253–279.

Keeter, Scott. 1987. "The Illusion of Intimacy: Television and the Role of Candidate Personal Qualities in Voter Choice." *Public Opinion Quarterly* 51 (Autumn): 344–358.

Keith, Bruce E., David B. Magleby, Candice J. Nelson, Elizabeth A. Orr, Mark C. Westlye, and Raymond E. Wolfinger. 1992. *The Myth of the Independent Voter*. Oakland: University of California Press.

Kellett, Janet B., Ronald H. Humphrey, and Randall G. Sleeth. 2002. "Empathy and Complex Task Performance: Two Routes to Leadership." *The Leadership Quarterly* 13: 523–544.

Kendall, Kathleen E. 1995. "The Problem of Beginnings in New Hampshire: Control over the Play." In *Presidential Campaign Discourse: Strategic Communication Problems*, ed. Kathleen E. Kendall, 1–34. Albany: State University of New York Press.

Kendall, Kathleen E. 2000. *Communication in the Presidential Primaries: Candidates and the Media, 1912–2000*. Westport, CT: Praeger.

Key, V. O. 1966. *The Responsible Electorate*. Cambridge, MA: Harvard University Press.

Kinder, Donald R. 1986. "Presidential Character Revisited." In *Political Cognition*, ed. Richard R. Lau and David O. Sears. Hillsdale, NJ: Erlbaum, 233–255.

Kinder, Donald R., and Nathan Kalmoe. 2016. *Neither Liberal nor Conservative: Ideological Innocence in the American Public*. Chicago: University of Chicago Press.

Kinder, Donald R., and Thomas R. Palfrey, eds. 1993. *Experimental Foundations of Political Science*. Ann Arbor: University of Michigan Press.

King, James D., and Jason B. McConnell. 2003. "The Effect of Negative Campaign Advertising on Vote Choice: The Mediating Influence of Gender." *Social Science Quarterly* 84(4): 843–857.

Klar, Samara, and Yanna Krupnikov. 2016. *Independent Politics: How American Disdain for Parties Leads to Political Inaction*. New York: Cambridge University Press.

Koch, Jeffrey W. 2000. "Do Citizens Apply Gender Stereotypes to Infer Candidates' Ideological Orientations?" *Journal of Politics* 62(2): 414–429.

Krupnikov, Yanna. 2011. "When Does Negativity Demobilize? Tracing the Conditional Effect of Negative Campaigning on Voter Turnout." *American Journal of Political Science* 55(4): 796812.

Kuklinski, James H., Paul J. Quirk, Jennifer Jerit, and Robert F. Rich. 2001. "The Political Environment and Citizen Competence." *American Journal of Political Science*, 45(2): 410–424.

Kuklinski, James H., Paul J. Quirk, Jennifer Jerit, David Schwieder, and Robert F. Rich. 2000. "Misinformation and the Currency of Democratic Citizenship." *Journal of Politics* 62(3): 790–816.

Kuklinski, James H. and Darrell M. West. 1981. "Economic Expectations and Voting Behavior in United States Senate and House Elections." *American Political Science Review* 75: 436–447.

Kunda, Ziva. 1990. "The Case for Motivated Reasoning." *Psychological Bulletin* 108(3): 480–498.

Lanoue, David J. 1994. "Retrospective and Prospective Voting in Presidential-Year Elections." *Political Research Quarterly* 47(1): 193–205.

Lau, Richard R., and Gerald Pomper. 2004. *Negative Campaigning: An Analysis of U.S. Senate Elections*. Lanham, MD: Rowman & Littlefield.

Lau, Richard R., and David P. Redlawsk. 2005. "Effects of Positive and Negative Political Advertisements on Information Processing." Unpublished manuscript, Rutgers University.

Lavine, Howard, Christopher Johnston, and Marco Steenbergen. 2012. *The Ambivalent Partisan: How Critical Loyalty Promote Democracy*. New York: Oxford University Press.

Lawless, Jennifer L. 2004. "Women, War and Winning Elections: Gender Stereotyping in the Post-September 11th Era." *Political Research Quarterly* 57(3): 479–490.

Lawless, Jennifer L., Sean M. Theriault, and Samantha Guthrie. 2018. "Nice Girls? Sex, Collegiality, and Bipartisan Cooperation in the US Congress." *Journal of Politics* 80(4): 1268–1282.

Lawrence, Regina G., and Melody Rose. 2010. *Hillary Clinton's Race for the White House: Gender Politics and the Media on the Campaign Trail*. Boulder, CO: Lynne Rienner.

Lawton, L. Dale, and Paul Freedman. 2001. "Beyond Negativity: Advertising Effects in the 2000 Virginia Senate Race." Presented at the annual meeting of the Midwest Political Science Association.

Layman, Geoff C. 1997. "Religion and Political Behavior in the United States: The Impact of Beliefs, Affiliations, and Commitment from 1980 to 1994." *Public Opinion Quarterly* 68: 288–316.

Lee, Frances E. 2016. *Insecure Majorities: Congress and the Perpetual Campaign*. Chicago: University of Chicago Press.

Lenz, Gabriel S. 2012. *Follow the Leader? How Voters Respond to Politicians' Performance and Policies*. Chicago: University of Chicago Press.

Lewis, Kristi. M. 2000. "When Leaders Display Emotion: How Followers Respond to Negative Emotional Expression of Male and Female Leaders." *Journal of Organizational Behavior* 21: 221–234.

Lockerbie, B. 1991. "Prospective Economic Voting in U.S. House Elections, 1956–88." *Legislative Studies Quarterly* 16: 239–261.

Lodge, Milton, and Charles S. Taber. 2013. *The Rationalizing Voter*. New York: Cambridge University Press.

Lord, Robert G., Olga Epitropaki, Roseanne J. Foti, and Tiffany Keller Hansbrough. 2020. "Implicit Leadership Theories, Implicit Followership Theories, and Dynamic Processing of Leadership Information." *Annual Review of Organizational Psychology and Organizational Behavior* 7: 49–74.

Lupia, Arthur. 1994. "Shortcuts Versus Encyclopedias: Information and Voting Behavior in California Insurance Reform Elections." *American Political Science Review* 88(1): 63–76.

Lyons, Jeffrey, and William P. Jaeger. 2014. "Who Do Voters Blame for Policy Failure? Information and the Partisan Assignment of Blame." *State Politics & Policy Quarterly* 14(3): 321–341.

MacKuen, Michael B., Robert S. Erickson, and James A. Stimson. 1992. "Peasants or Bankers? The American Electorate and the U.S. Economy." *American Political Science Review* 86: 597–611.

Maestas, Cherie D., Lonna Rae Atkeson, Thomas Croom, and Lisa A. Bryant. 2008. "Shifting the Blame: Federalism, Media and Public Assignment of Blame Following Hurricane Katrina." *Publius: The Journal of Federalism* 38(4): 609–632.

Mansbridge, Jane. 1999. "Should Blacks Represent Blacks and Women Represent Women? A Contingent 'Yes.'" *Journal of Politics* 61(3): 628–657.

Mason, Lilliana. 2018. *Uncivil Agreement: How Politics Became Our Identity*. Chicago: University of Chicago Press.

Mason, Lilliana. 2013. "Smells Like Team Spirit: How Partisan Sorting and Identity Polarize Political Behavior." Presented at the New York Area Political Psychology Workshop, November 16, 2013.

Mason, Lilliana. 2014. "'I Disrespectfully Agree': The Differential Effects of Partisan Sorting on Behavioral and Issue Polarization." *American Journal of Political Science* 59(1): 128–145.

Mason, Lilliana, and Julie Wronski. 2018. "One Tribe to Bind Them All: How Our Social Group Attachments Strengthen Partisanship." *Political Psychology* 39(S1): 257–277.

Mayhew, David. 1974. *Congress: The Electoral Connection*. New Haven, CT: Yale University Press.

McCann, James A. 1990. "Changing Electoral Contexts and Changing Candidate Images During the 1984 Presidential Campaign." *American Politics Quarterly* 18 (Apr.): 123–140.

McDermott, Monika L. 1998. "Race and Gender Cues in Low-Information Elections." *Political Research Quarterly*. 51(4): 895–918.

McDermott, Monika L. 2005. "Candidate Occupations and Voter Information Shortcuts." *Journal of Politics* 67(1): 201–219.

McDonald, Jared. 2020. "Avoiding the Hypothetical: Why 'Mirror Experiments' Are an Essential Part of Survey Research." *International Journal of Public Opinion Research* 32(2): 266–283.

McDonald, Jared. 2021. "Who Cares? Explaining Perceptions of Compassion in Candidates for Office." *Political Behavior* 43: 1371–1394.

McDonald, Jared, David Karol, and Lilliana Mason. 2020. "'An Inherited Money Dude from Queens County': How Unseen Candidate Characteristics Affect Voter Perceptions." *Political Behavior* 42: 915–938.

McKee, John P., and Alex C. Sheriffs. 1957. "The Differential Evaluation of Males and Females." *Journal of Personality* 25(3): 356–371.

McThomas, Mary, and Michael Tesler. 2016. "The Growing Influence of Gender Attitudes on Public Support for Hillary Clinton, 2018–2012." *Politics and Gender* 12(1): 28–49.

Mercer, Philip. 1972. *Sympathy and Ethics*. Oxford: Clarendon Press.

Miller, Arthur H., Patricia Gurin, Gerald Gurin, and Oksana Malanchuk. 1981. "Group Consciousness and Political Participation." *American Journal of Political Science* 25(3): 494–511.

Miller, Arthur H., Martin P. Wattenberg, and Oksana Malanchuk. 1986. "Schematic Assessments of Presidential Candidates." *American Political Science Review* 80 (June): 521–540.

Miller, Warren E., and J. Merrill Shanks. 1996. *The New American Voter*. Cambridge, MA: Harvard University Press.

Milyo, Jeffrey, and Samantha Schosberg. 2000. "Gender bias and selection bias in House elections." *Public Choice* 105(1): 41–59.

Mutz, Diana. 2006. *Hearing the Other Side*. Cambridge: Cambridge University Press.

Nagel, Thomas. 1970. *The Possibility of Altruism*. Oxford: Clarendon Press.

Neiman, Jayme L., Frank J. Gonzalez, Kevin Wilkinson, Kevin B. Smith, and John R. Hibbing 2016. "Speaking Different Languages or Reading from the Same Script? Value-Based Word Usage of Democratic and Republican Politicians." *Political Communication* 33(2): 212–240.

Newcomb, Theodore M. 1956. "The Prediction of Interpersonal Attraction." *American Psychologist* 11(11): 575–586.

Niemi, Richard G., and Herbert F. Weisberg. 1976. "Are Parties Becoming Irrelevant?" In *Controversies in American Voting Behavior*, ed. Richard G. Niemi and Herbert F. Weisberg. San Francisco: W.H. Freeman.

Niven, David. 2005. "Issue Related Learning in a Gubernatorial Campaign: A Panel Study." Unpublished manuscript, Florida Atlantic University.

Niven, David. 2006. "A Field Experiment on the Effects of Negative Campaign Mail on Voter Turnout in a Municipal Election." *Political Research Quarterly* 59(2): 203–210.

Nook, Eric C., Desmond C. Ong, Sylvia A. Morelli, Jason P. Mitchell, and Jamil Zaki. 2016. "Prosocial Conformity: Prosocial Norms Generalize Across Behavior and Empathy." *Personality and Social Psychology Bulletin* 42(8): 1045–1062.

Nussbaum, Martha. 1996. *For Love of Country: Debating the Limits of Patriotism*. Boston: Beacon Press.

Nyhan, Brendan, Ethan Porter, Jason Reifler, and Thomas J. Wood. 2020. "Taking Corrections Literally but Not Seriously? The Effects of Information on Factual Beliefs and Candidate Favorability." *Political Behavior* 42: 939–960.

Nyhan, Brendan, and Jason Reifler. 2010. "When Corrections Fail: The Persistence of Political Misperceptions." *Political Behavior* 32(2): 303–330.

Palmer, Barbara, and Dennis Simon. 2010. *Breaking the political glass ceiling: Women and congressional elections*. New York: Routledge.

Phoenix, Davin. 2019. *The Anger Gap: How Race Shapes Emotion in Politics*. New York: Cambridge University Press.

Piston, Spencer 2010. "How Explicit Racial Prejudice Hurt Obama in the 2008 Election." *Political Behavior* 34(2): 431–451.

Piston, Spencer. 2018. *Class Attitudes in America: Sympathy for the Poor, Resentment of the Rich, and Political Implications*. New York: Cambridge University Press.

Pitkin, Hanna. 1967. *The Concept of Representation*. Los Angeles: University of California Press.

Popkin, Samuel L. 1994. *The Reasoning Voter: Communication and Persuasion in Presidential Campaigns*. Chicago: University of Chicago Press.

Potter, Rachel Augustine, and Craig Volden. 2021. "A Female Policy Premium? Agency Context and Women's Leadership in the US Federal Bureaucracy." *Journal of Public Administration Research and Theory* 31(1): 91–107.

Redlawsk, David P. 2002. "Hot Cognition or Cool Consideration? Testing the Effects of Motivated Reasoning on Political Decision Making." *Journal of Politics* 64(4): 1021–1044.

Riccucci, Norma M., Gregg G. Van Ryzin, and Cecilia F. Lavena. 2014. "Representative Bureaucracy in Policing: Does It Increase Perceived Legitimacy?" *Journal of Public Administration Research and Theory* 24(3): 537–551.

Riccucci, Norma M., Gregg G. Van Ryzin, and Huafang Li. 2016. "Representative Bureaucracy and the Willingness to Coproduce: An Experimental Study." *Public Administration Review* 76(1): 121–130.

Ridgeway, Cecilia L. 2011 *Framed by Gender: How Gender Inequality Persists in the Modern World.* New York: Oxford University Press.

Rouse, Stella. 2013. *Latinos in the Legislative Process.* New York: Cambridge University Press.

Rudman, Laurie A. 1998. "Self-promotion as a risk factor for women: The costs and benefits of counterstereotypical impression management." Journal of Personality and Social Psychology 74(3): 629–645.

Rudman, Laurie A., Corrine A. Moss-Racusin, Julie E. Phelan, and Sanne Nauts. 2012. "Status incongruity and backlash effects: Defending the gender hierarchy motivates prejudice against female leaders." *Journal of Experimental Social Psychology* 48: 165-179.

Rudolph, Thomas J. 2003. "Who's Responsible for the Economy? The Formation and Consequences of Responsibility Attributions." *American Journal of Political Science* 47(4): 697–712.

Sanbonmatsu, Kira. 2002. Gender Stereotypes and Vote Choice." *American Journal of Political Science* 46(1): 20–34.

Sanchez, Gabriel R., and Edward D. Vargas. 2016. "Taking a Closer Look at Identity: The Link Between Theory and Measurement of Group Consciousness and Linked Fate." *Political Research Quarterly* 69(1): 160–174.

Schuessler, Alexander A. 2000. *A Logic of Expressive Choice.* Princeton: Princeton University Press.

Schwarz, Norbert, and Herbert Bless. 1992. "Assimilation and Contrast Effects in Attitude Measurement: An Inclusion/Exclusion Model." *Advances in Consumer Research* 19: 72–77.

Scott, Zachary A. 2021. "Lost in the Crowd: The Effect of Volatile Fields on Presidential Primaries." *American Politics Research* 49(2): 221–232.

Shen, Fuyuan, and H. Denis Wu. 2002. "Effects of Soft-Money Issue Advertisements on Candidate Evaluation and Voting Preference: An Exploration." *Mass Communication & Society* 5(4): 395–410.

Simien, Evelyn M. 2005. "Race, Gender, and Linked Fate." *Journal of Black Studies* 35(5): 529–550.

Slote, Michael. 2001. *Morals from Motives.* Oxford: Oxford University Press.

Smith, Hedrick. 1988. *The Power Game: How Washington Works.* New York: Random House.

Stimson, James A. 1991. *Public Opinion in America: Moods, Cycles, and Swings.* Boulder, CO: Westview Press.

Stivers, Camilla. 2002. *Gender Images in Public Administration: Legitimacy and the Administrative State.* Thousand Oaks, CA: Sage.

Stout, Christopher T., Kelsey Kretschmer, and Leah Ruppanner. 2017. "Gender Linked Fate, Race/Ethnicity, and the Marriage Gap in American Politics." *Political Research Quarterly* 70(3): 509–522.

Sullivan, John L., John H. Aldrich, Eugene Borgida, and Wendy M. Rahn. 1990. "Candidate Appraisal and Human Nature: Man and Superman in the 1984 Election." *Political Psychology* 11 (Sept.): 459–484.

Swain, Carol M. 1993. *Black Faces, Black Interests: The Representation of African Americans in Congress*. Cambridge, MA: Harvard University Press.

Taber, Charles S., and Milton Lodge. 2006. "Motivated Skepticism in the Evaluation of Political Beliefs." *American Journal of Political Science* 50(3): 755–769.

Tajfel, Henri, M. G. Billig, R. P. Bundy, and Claude Flament. 1971. "Social Categorization and Intergroup Behavior." *European Journal of Social Psychology* 1(2): 149–178.

Tate, Katherine. 1993. *From Protest to Politics: The New Black Voters in American Elections*. Cambridge, MA: Harvard University Press.

Tate, Katherine. 2003. *Black Faces in the Mirror: African Americans and Their Representatives in the U.S. Congress*. Princeton: Princeton University Press.

Theiss-Morse. 2009. *Who Counts as an American? The Boundaries of National Identity*. New York: Cambridge University Press.

Thorson, Esther, Ekaterina Ognianova, James Coyle, and Frank Denton. 2000. "Negative Political Ads and Negative Citizen Orientations toward Politics." *Journal of Current Issues & Research in Advertising* 22 (Spring): 13–41.

Underwood, Bill, and Bert Moore. 1982. "Perspective-Taking and Altruism." *Psychological Bulletin* 91(1): 143–173.

Uslaner, Eric M., 2008. "The Foundations of Trust: Macro and Micro." *Cambridge Journal of Economics* 32: 289–294.

Weaver, R. Kent. 1986. "The Politics of Blame Avoidance." *Journal of Public Policy* 6(4): 371–398.

Wood, Thomas, and Ethan Porter. 2018. "The Elusive Backfire Effect: Mass Attitudes' Steadfast Factual Adherence." *Political Behavior* 40(1): 1–29.

Winter, Nicholas J. G. 2010. "Masculine Republicans and Feminine Democrats: Gender and Americans' Explicit and Implicit Images of the Political Parties." *Political Behavior* 32(4): 587–618.

Wispé, Lauren. 1986. "The Distinction Between Sympathy and Empathy: To Call Forth a Concept, a Word Is Needed." *Journal of Personality and Social Psychology* 50(2): 314–321.

Yukl, Gary A. 1998. *Leadership in Organizations*. 4th ed. Upper Saddle River, NJ: Prentice Hall.

Zaki, Jamil. 2014. "Empathy: A Motivated Account." *Psychological Bulletin* 140: 1608–1647.

Zaller, John. 1992. *The Nature and Origins of Mass Opinion*. Cambridge: Cambridge University Press.

Zemojtel-Piotrowska, Magdalena A., Alison Marganski, Tomasz Baran, and Jaroslaw Piotrowski. 2017. "Corruption and Sexual Scandal: The Importance of Politician Gender." *Anales de Psicología* 33(1): 133–141.

Zhao, Kun, Eamonn Ferguson, and Luke D. Smillie. 2017. "When Fair is Not Equal: Compassion and Politeness Predict Allocations of Wealth Under Different Norms of Equity and Need." *Social Psychological and Personality Science* 8(8): 847–857.

Index

For the benefit of digital users, indexed terms that span two pages (e.g., 52–53) may, on occasion, appear on only one of those pages.

Tables and figures are indicated by *t* and *f* following the page number

"Sesame Street" (television program), 161, 162
shared emotion, 7
Sheinkopf, Hank, 28–29
She Should Run (advocacy group), 166
similarity–attraction effect, 64–65
sincerity barrier, 61–63, 81–82
Sleeth, Randall G., 61
smear campaigns. *See* character attacks
social media, 27
sociopolitical sorting, 11–12, 83–84
Survey Sampling International (SSI), 69, 69n.22, 72, 96–98, 98*t*, 99*t*
Swers, Michele L., 126
sympathy
defined, 5–7, 59–60
empathy versus, 5–7, 57–61, 72–74, 73*f*, 74*f*, 121

Taylor, Breanna, 1
Teflon hypothesis
generally, 144, 149
Hillary Clinton and, 151–53
independent voters and, 153–54
partisanship and, 153–55
research study, 149–50
Theiss-Morse, Elizabeth, 23
Theriault, Sean M., 166–67
trait ownership, 34
Trump, Donald
generally, 19–20
anger and, 9–10, 10*f*, 93–94
Biden and, 57–58
blue-collar voters and, 8–9, 14
compassion and, 3, 8, 14
conservatism and, 27
COVID-19 pandemic and, 1
Democratic Compassion Advantage and, 38–39

emotional empathy and, 7–11, 77, 79, 81
experiential empathy and, 4
Hillary Clinton and, 150, 151–52, 154, 155–56
Obama and, 148
Romney and, 150, 153
shared emotion and, 7
social media and, 27
surprising nature of election, 8
tax returns of, 144
voter dissatisfaction and, 75–76
vote totals of, 8, 19–20
white identity and, 10–11
Twitter, 27

Van Hollen, Chris, 42–45, 44*f*, 45*f*, 46*f*, 89

Warren, Elizabeth, 109
Washington Post–University of Maryland (poll), 43, 51–53, 53*t*, 149, 157–58, 159*t*, 160*t*
Webster, Steven, 56
Wehby, Monica, 109–10, 111
white identity, 10–11
Williams, Dave, 7, 8
Windett, Jason Harold, 166
women
challenges faced by women candidates, 166
Democratic Party and, 109–10
gender, compassion and (*see* gender, compassion and)
gender bias, 166–67
implications of study for women seeking elected office, 166–67
partisan polarization and, 166–67
Republican Party and, 109–10
transformational approach, 166–67